IT'S NOT THE HEAT, IT'S THE HUMIDITY

*Seventh in the Series of Stories About Growing Up
in and Around Small Towns in the Midwest*

Edited by
Jean Tennant

Shapato Publishing, LLC
Everly, Iowa

Published by: Shapato Publishing, LLC
PO Box 476
Everly, Iowa 51338

ISBN-13: 978-0692300275
ISBN-10: 0692300279

Library of Congress Control Number: 2014952267

First Printing November 2014

Cover photo: Margaret Degnan Dau

"I was raised on a little farm about twelve miles out of Portsmouth, Ohio. I can truthfully say farm life is the best thing that can happen to a kid."

Roy Rogers

John & Karen,

We hope you enjoy all of these stories.

Ken

Dec 2014

Photo provided by Jean Tennant

TABLE OF CONTENTS

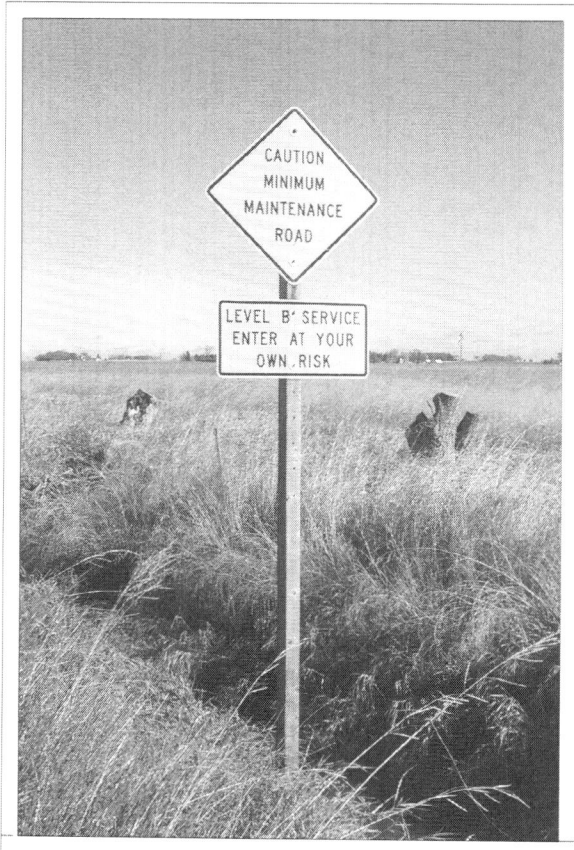

IT'S NOT THE HEAT,
IT'S THE
HUMIDITY

*Seventh in the Series of Stories About Growing Up
in and Around Small Towns in the Midwest*

Photo Provided by Orville Taylor

A LUCKY GUY IN GRIM TIMES
Orville Taylor

In the fall of '41, I was a high school senior involved in the usual high school activities. Conflicts and unrest existed throughout the world; then on December 7, our lives changed abruptly. The Japanese bombed Pearl Harbor, our country was at war, and the draft was reinstated. The twelve guys in my senior class were all 18, and we wondered how soon we'd be drafted and how many of us would survive.

As soon as we finished high school, my brother, Glen, and I reported for physicals at Camp Dodge in Des Moines. Because he'd lost sight in one eye in a BB gun accident, Glen didn't pass. I did, but to my surprise, along with three classmates, I received a II-C classification: Deferred for Farming.

I was lucky to have my II-C classification and did what I could to deserve it. Always aware of what servicemen were going through and wary of comments about draft dodgers, I spent most of my time working at home or harvesting for neighbors with two-row equipment. One year the Department of Agriculture issued me a plaque stating I'd harvested 600 acres, third in the state.

In December of 1944, the Germans broke through allied defenses in Belgium at the Battle of the Bulge. Duane Newman, one of my classmates, lost his life in that conflict, and my classification changed to 1-A: Available, Fit for Military Service. After another physical at Fort Snelling, Minnesota, on January 27, 1945, I was sent to Fort Riley, Kansas for inoculations, then to Fort Joseph T. Robinson, near Little Rock, Arkansas for basic training.

Sixteen weeks of basic included calisthenics, marching, rifle and bayonet training, and maneuvers. My left foot suffered a stress fracture from marching up Clifton Mountain with a full pack and my M1 rifle. A steel support in my shoe solved the discomfort and training continued. We pitched tents for bivouac, an outdoor encampment, the last two weeks. Rainy days were supposedly good training, as wars don't stop for weather conditions. When I asked an officer where I could find the latrine, he pointed to a tree and said, "That's the officers' tree. Use any other one you wish."

Following a short furlough, I was on to Fort Ord, California, where thousands of troops were coming in and going out every day. With other non-swimmers, I was assigned five swimming lessons. The fifth would be a jump from a 20-foot tower wearing a life jacket. Those who wouldn't jump in were thrown in. I made up my mind I'd jump, but luck was with me; we moved out after my fourth lesson.

When we left Fort Ord our destination was secret; no letters or phone calls allowed. Not one who liked to follow orders, I did write to my parents during the two-day trip to Seattle. As a serviceman, I was entitled to write *Free* in place of a stamp on military stationery, so I tossed my letter from a train window in some small Oregon town, hoping someone would send it on. About a month later, my parents received the beat-up, rain-damaged, but readable letter.

The Red Cross provided coffee and doughnuts, and a band played "Sentimental Journey" as we sailed from Seattle in July. I didn't usually drink coffee, but the doughnuts were dry, and I needed it for dunking.

Because we'd been issued long johns and woolen uniforms, we thought we were going to the Aleutians. A few days out, heavy uniforms were exchanged for lighter ones. Our destination was Eniwetok to join a convoy headed for Okinawa and on to the invasion of Japan.

At Eniwetok, we watched taxpayers' money go up in smoke when the woolen uniforms were piled and burned, but more surprising events awaited us. On August 6, a single bomb destroyed the city of Hiroshima. Two days later another destroyed Nagasaki. At the Emperor's command, the Japanese turned in their weapons. Instead of taking part in an invasion, I became part of the occupation.

My first assignment was checking bases and schools around Wakamatsu for remaining armaments. We found none, but learned that students down to fifth grade had been trained with weapons and explosives. For the rest of my tour, I guarded cargo ships and warehouses in Yokohama. Because the military was segregated at the time, Black soldiers drove trucks, Japanese workers unloaded cargo, and white soldiers guarded it.

Once, while guarding cargo in the hold, Japanese workers attempted to drop an oak hatch-cover on my head. Hatch-covers are six by three feet, and three inches thick. The cover hit my rifle, scraped my shoulder, and slammed to the floor. I picked up my fully-loaded rifle and looked up to see six apologetic Japanese workers bowing to me. I didn't fire.

Requirements demanded clean uniforms daily. That was difficult since we were each issued only two. On guard duty one night, I found uniforms my size and "moonlight requisitioned" three more pairs of pants and three shirts. After that I always had clean uniforms, as I sent two at a time to the laundry.

We were each issued one carton of cigarettes a week. I didn't smoke, so passed them up at first. When I learned cigarettes were good for barter with the Japanese, I took my share. I was also entitled to buy a six-pack of beer each week. I didn't drink either, but found the beer to be a sensible investment. I doubled my money by selling it to other GIs when they ran out.

I sent most of my bartered and purchased items home. Among the souvenirs were two rifles with bayonets, a Samurai sword, Hari-Kari knives, a parasol, items of silk clothing, a hundred yards of white silk, and a Japanese baseball that is smaller than ours. I also paid a local artist to paint Mt. Fuji on the back of my field jacket.

In the spring, companies formed baseball teams, and I wrote home for my glove. Out of 200 men in each company, twelve were chosen to play. I was one of the lucky ones and volunteered for guard duty at night, so I could play ball during the day. Two different chances for promotions, involving job changes, came my way. The first was a cook's helper. I turned that down quickly. The second was taking charge of the auxiliary light-plant motor. It was an easy job, but taking it would cut into my baseball time. I chose to remain a PFC.

I was about twenty miles from Tokyo and visited there at times. About half of that city had been destroyed. On one visit, I registered at a Red Cross building. Later a school friend, Herluf Thomsen, visited the same place, found my name, and managed to look me up. It was great to see someone from home.

When our time was up, 5,200 of us boarded an old luxury liner and headed home. We disembarked in Oakland, California, on my 23rd birthday, September 29, 1946. From there, we went to Chicago for processing and a final inspection. I was told I couldn't keep the field jacket with Mount Fuji on the back, because it was altered. Stepping out of line, I folded it, put it in my field pack, set it aside, and got back in line. After passing inspection, I picked up my field pack, stuffed it in my duffle bag and left.

Unfortunately, they didn't find the cartridge for a Japanese rifle I'd sent home. It was hidden in my boot. . . .

On my first Sunday at home I took some of my friends out to the grove to watch me fire one of the Japanese rifles. Unaware that someone had tampered with the gun, I set up a target, aimed, fired and set off an explosion. Luckily, it missed my eyes, but my forehead caught powder burns and at least a dozen brass particles. One by one, our family doctor picked them out and bandaged my forehead.

As for the twelve guys in my senior class, one served in the Air Force, two in the Navy, six in the Army, and three didn't pass their physicals. There was one loss of life, and no other casualties.

The souvenirs were put to use. My sister, a niece, and my wife wore wedding dresses made from the white silk, and another niece's baptismal dress was sewn from the fabric. Grandsons played Ninjas in silk pajamas; the parasol and kimono are for my granddaughters; my son will get the baseball and other items; the painted field jacket hangs in a museum in Hartley, Iowa; and a few years ago, I sold the sword and knives for over $800. Not a bad return for the cigarettes and beer.

Prior to his army years, **Orville Taylor** never strayed far from home. His experiences taught him the value of travel, a pastime he continued to pursue. He farmed, was involved with mining in Mexico, sold securities, and operated an antique shop with his wife, Betty. At age ninety-one, he still refinishes furniture, sells at antique shows, and loves to reminisce. He enjoys his grandchildren and works with a local historical society.

Photo of Cheyenne Hibbing,
provided by Betty Taylor

Betty Eeten
Photo provided by the Hartley Historical Society

Betty Eeten, 1988 Hartley Threshing Days Queen
Photo provided by the Hartley Historical Society

BETTY EETEN VS BETTY CROCKER
Connie Olhausen

It was my pleasure to know Betty Eeten as a dear friend and fellow registered nurse for more than fifty years. The first ten of those years were in the employment of Drs. Peterson and Brown, where we were both staff nurses, and then in the former Hand Hospital. The hospital was located on the corner of Central Avenue and Maple Drive in Hartley, Iowa, now the location of City Hall.

Betty had preceded me on staff after having previously served as a navy nurse during World War II and the Korean Conflict. During her tour of service, she had served for a time under one Commander Black, the husband of a well-known child actress by the name of Shirley Temple.

Betty told the story of answering the phone one evening while serving at the base hospital. Shirley Temple Black was the caller, and her message was simply, "I think my baby is coming."

Betty didn't give any details of the subsequent labor and delivery. Instead, in true "Betty style," she seemed to regard assisting in the delivery of Shirley Temple's baby as all in a day's—or perhaps more accurately—a night's work.

Betty was a delightful, caring person with few if any complaints and an easy, unmistakable hearty laugh. As I reflect on her nature, it seemed that she simply accepted life as it was, without expressing a desire for anything different or better.

As nurses, we encountered each other at work as I was going off-duty and she was coming on. I worked the evening shift until 11:00 PM, and Betty worked nights or the "graveyard shift" as it was called by many.

It seemed those hours suited her well, because babies have a habit of arriving at night, and Betty was definitely a baby person. She was in her element when assisting expectant moms in labor and delivery, or when caring for the newborn infants. Many times over the ensuing years, women who had been new moms during Betty's tenure have told me how comforting and reassuring it was to have Betty with them during their labor and delivery experience.

Another story that comes to mind involving Betty didn't occur in the hospital setting, but rather in the kitchen of the home where she and her husband Harry lived, across from Pleasant View Cemetery in Hartley. I happened to stop in one day when Betty was mixing a "made from scratch" angel food cake.

As a young bride, I considered myself something of an expert in crafting from-scratch angel food cakes, because my mother-in-law, Leona Olhausen, had given me a Betty Crocker cookbook at a bridal shower. It was my only cookbook, and I considered it the bible of superior recipes and infallible methods.

Betty Crocker's instructions for the correct method of transferring the angel food cake batter to the baking pan was to carefully place it in the pan, gently run a knife through it several times to release trapped air, and then gently place it in a preheated oven.

You can imagine my reaction of shock and horror as a different Betty—Betty Eeten this time—slammed her filled cake pan on the edge of the table. Twice.

"What are you doing?" I gasped.

To which she replied, "Getting the air out."

Still in shock, I said, "My Betty Crocker cookbook says to run a knife through the batter to get the air out."

With that, she banged the pan on the table edge one more time, possibly as a show of contempt for Betty Crocker and her methods.

After that, whenever angel food cake came up in conversation, Betty would laughingly inquire as to whether I had ever tried banging the cake pan on the table before placing it in the oven.

As a true disciple of Betty Crocker, I never have, and am quite certain I never will.

Connie Olhausen has lived in the Hartley, Iowa area her entire life. She is a retired nurse-anesthetist with many interests and activities; including antiques, quilting, golfing, and church and community involvement. In the past few years, her interests have expanded to focus on The Hartley Historical Society and the restoration of the Patch/Eeten House, a Victorian home built in the 1890s. Betty Eeten was the granddaughter of early owner, Frank Patch. She was the last occupant of the home.

Photo provided by Kent Stephens

July 1960

Kent, driving a Farmall
"H" tractor with baler
and hay wagon.

At Osceola, Iowa on the
farm owned by my
grandparents in 1915.

MY FIRST TRIP TO FIPPS' GARAGE
Kent Stephens

D riving tractors is one of my most favorite things ever, but baling hay is just downright BORING.

It was the summer of 1960, I was a ten-year-old suburban kid from Northern California and this was my first time working on the family farm with my Uncle Clarence, just west of Osceola, Iowa. Clarence quickly taught me how to do all of the farm chores including feeding and watering the cattle, sheep, hogs and chickens. He also taught me how to properly and safely operate his Case VAC tractor so I could mow weeds in the pasture. Later I learned to rake and bale hay. I loved mowing and raking as those were high-speed, third-gear operations, but baling was more complex, slow and tedious. It was pure first gear drudgery. I tried to convince my uncle that hauling hay wagons back and forth to the barn would be a better use of my time and skills, but Clarence firmly told me it was all part of the job and baling was my assignment. I would rather clean my room than bale hay. Well, not really.

One July afternoon we finished the baling much earlier than I thought we would. The hay was in the barn and it wasn't even three o'clock. Uncle Clarence told me to wash up, put on a clean shirt and get in the pickup. We were going to town. Town? On a weekday when there was still daylight? I kept my mouth shut and didn't ask questions.

Soon we were pulling into Fipps' garage and gas station. I never knew what the real business name of the garage was. Everyone just called it Fipps' for the man who ran it.

Fipps' garage was quite weathered and hadn't seen a paint brush for many years. The driveways and lot were gravel and there were only two old gas pumps: regular and ethyl. There was no indoor plumbing; the "clean restrooms" was a little wooden building out back. The garage had a heavily worn and oil-stained wooden plank floor. Just inside the front door were the cash register and five or six mismatched chairs. These were all arranged in a haphazard, Knights of the Roundtable circle.

That afternoon there was a lot of social activity, with most of the chairs occupied. Some of the local farmers were having involved discussions covering every imaginable topic from politics to the price of cattle, hogs, fertilizer, corn and soybeans. The most discussed topic was the weather. Hot, cold, wet or dry, it was always the weather.

Along the wall there was a chest-type freezer box that was painted a bright fire engine red with white accents and script lettering that said Coca~Cola. Inside the box were parallel steel tracks holding bottles in a rack system. Each row held bottles with unique and different colored bottle caps. Back home my parents never bought bottled drinks and I had never had a soda pop. I think I had heard of Coca~Cola, but I was pretty sure it was a drink only for adults.

Clarence called me over and gave me three nickels and said, "Get Fipps and I a Coke and then get what you want for yourself."

I approached the Coca~Cola machine with much trepidation. It was a contraption that I had never before operated. I lifted the lid, observed the bottle racks and identified the two rows of Coke. In those days there were no such things as Diet, Caffeine Free, Lime, Cherry, Vanilla, New or Classic, or even cans, plastic bottles, or anything of the sort.

I put the first nickel in the slot and let'er go, I heard it click through the trip mechanism and then *thunk* into the coin box. I gently guided the first bottle through the metal rack maze, to the rubber dispense flapper. I pulled up, as the instructions said. The flapper did not want to release easily, and the serrations around the edge of the metal bottle cap cut into my fingers. I let go of the bottle before the flapper tripped. Rats! This was trickier than it looked and on top of that I realized you only get one attempt at the flapper! The first nickel was gone, with nothing to show for it except for my newfound experience.

I was a fast learner though, and I got the next two bottles out without incident. I gave Fipps and Clarence their drinks. Clarence asked where my drink was. I had to tell him what happened. I didn't expect to get a drink as I had wasted a nickel. I would have liked to try my first soda pop, but it wasn't going to

15

be this time. Then I saw Clarence nod to Fipps. Fipps reached up on the little ledge above the cash drawer and retrieved another nickel and gave it to me.

Back to the machine, I now had a new problem. Lifting the lid again, I was faced with a difficult choice. I didn't think I was supposed to drink Coca~Cola, but the next item in the rack was Root Beer! I didn't know what that was either, but I knew I shouldn't be drinking any kind of beer. In the last track the bottles had an orange and white cap labeled Bireley's Orange. I could barely see the contents of the bottle, but it looked somewhat like orange juice. I was in uncharted territory here, but I figured an orange drink would be safe enough. I dropped my nickel in the slot, negotiated the flapper and pulled out an ice cold bottle of Bireley's Orange Soda.

I popped the cap and took a slug. It was cold, orangey, and sweet. I learned later that Bireley's was not carbonated, but pasteurized with real fruit juices, so it was kind of like Hi-Test orange juice. I went back over by Clarence and Fipps and sat on a case of oil and listened to the men's conversation.

I was in Osceola, far from home, sitting in Fipps' garage, having my first soda pop with the guys. I felt like the luckiest kid in the world.

I baled hundreds of bales of hay that summer. We didn't always go into Fipps' garage for a soda afterwards, but often we did. Each trip was a new and wonderful adventure for me. Clarence believed in the saying "All work and no play..." and no matter how hard we worked, Clarence always managed to fit in some play for us. It was OK to take a break, but only if you earned it first. I often wondered if Clarence got in trouble with my mom for introducing me to soda pop, but I never heard anything about it.

I was a teenager before I decided to finally try Coca~Cola. What an experience that was! But that's an entirely different story.

Kent Stephens was born and raised in Northern California, but spent most every summer of his youth working on family farms around Osceola and Centerville, Iowa. Now retired from a diverse career in transportation, he lives with his wife, Kimberly, in Reno, Nevada. He spends his free time archiving family stories, photos and movies to print and DVDs for the rest of the family.

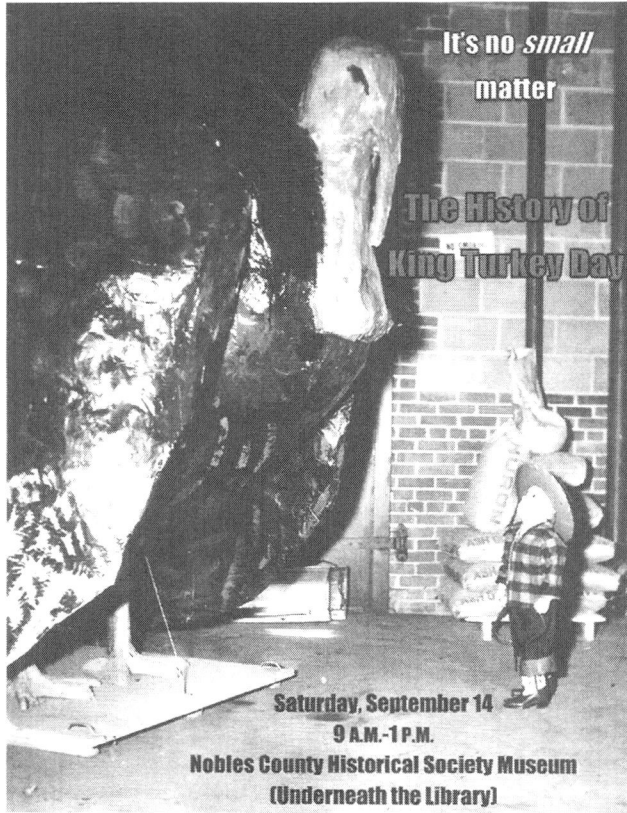

It's no *small* matter

The History of King Turkey Day

Saturday, September 14
9 A.M.-1 P.M.
Nobles County Historical Society Museum
(Underneath the Library)

Photo courtesy of Nobles County Minnesota Historical Society

WORTHINGTON, MINNESOTA
SEPTEMBER 1966

Scott Rubsam

It wasn't his dazzling smile I fell in love with at first. It was his sexy-rexy accent. He was from Boston, and that voice was exotic, yet American. Unintelligible, yet soothing. Loud and booming, yet also somehow quiet.

It was a smart voice. Smart and efficient. Smarter than all the rest of us combined. Smart like a man who knew who he was.

Robert Kennedy was the Attorney General of the United States, brother of the President of the United States. It was his job as Attorney General that brought him to Worthington, Minnesota, on that hot, sunny fall day.

You see, Worthington was, at that time, and still claims to be, the Turkey Capital of the World. It was the weekend of the town's annual celebration, Turkey Days. People flocked from all over to watch the parade, ride the rides, lose their money pitching pennies on the Midway, partake of the pancake feed, and, at noon, listen to the speakers.

Our school band had just finished marching in the parade. It was unusually hot for mid-September and our band uniforms were heavy wool. We were dripping with sweat. Wanting to change. Wanting some water. Wanting to eat. Wanting to kill. Beware the hungry, hot middle-schooler with too many wants.

But that accent, that voice stopped me in my tracks. I heard it over the town-square loudspeaker. I don't even remember what he was saying. Something about foreign policies, something very worldly, regarding Asia's food problems and what we could do, as Americans, to stop it. My stomach growled. I just wanted something to eat. But gradually he started speaking to me on my level, rather than over my head. So I stopped to listen. And gradually, bit by Massachusetts-spoken bit, I understood what he was saying. He had a knack for making you feel important, of including you in his ideas.

I listened to the whole speech. Then it ended. Over in fifteen minutes, and he was gone. But I was hooked. I was ready to man those plantations of Chinese corn. But for now, I had to have more of him.

I suspected he would leave by the back of the courthouse. And sure enough, as I raced around the corner, there he was, getting into the back of a baby-blue convertible, still signing autographs as the driver gunned the engine.

I was frantic. I had to get an autograph, some physical token that he had actually been here. But I had no paper, no pen. I looked around on the ground. The only thing I saw was a satin ring case, no doubt discarded from the Midway. It was dirty, with hardly any kind of a flat space for writing, but it would have to do.

I don't know what possessed me that day. Normally I was a shy person who would hang out at the back of a crowd. But on that day I pushed my way through.

He was in the convertible, which was starting to move, though slowly. I grabbed a pen from an old man standing next to me and thrust it and the ring case at Robert Kennedy. He looked at the ring case and my heart sank. What was I thinking? Surely he thought it was stupid. And it was. *He's not going to sign it*, I thought—but it was my only chance.

Then he looked at me and smiled. One of those dazzling, hypnotic Kennedy smiles. Eye-to-eye, and heart-to-heart. He scribbled something on the ring case before tossing it back to me, and the car sped away.

"Hey, that's my pen," the old man grumbled.

But I didn't care about any old pen. I was in seventh heaven. Looking down, there it was: "Best wishes, Bobby Kennedy."

Bobby. Not Robert—too formal. Not Bob—too informal. But Bobby. Like we were friends. Equals. Maybe even related.

Bobby. It was just right. As though he were talking directly to me. I clutched my memento as the sun poured down on the moment. It was a great day to be alive.

The following June, Bobby Kennedy—not Robert, not Bob, but Bobby Kennedy—would be dead. Felled by an assassin's bullet. That smile struck down forever. I was at band practice when I heard the news. I put down my clarinet and walked from the room, too sad that day for any music. I knew then that our world, myself included, would forever be changed.

If you travel to Boston and have the wonderful experience of going to the John F. Kennedy Library, you learn not only about JFK, but you can also view a short movie about Robert Kennedy, as well as another film regarding Martin Luther King. And you realize how, in a matter of a few short years, our country fell to its knees in violence. Held hostage by guns, guns and more guns. Enough said.

Our childhood bends behind us, constantly weaving its way in and out of our lives. And even though we say goodbye, we don't really.

Do we?

Scott M. Rubsam is an internationally known stage director who most recently directed Academy Award winner Ellen Burstyn and *Saturday Night Live* star Rachel Dratch in the world premiere of *Mean* in New York City. He is currently on the faculty of Metropolitan State University, where he has taught Directed Readings for the Stage (an on line dramatic literature course), Playwriting II, Directing I, and Women in Theatre.

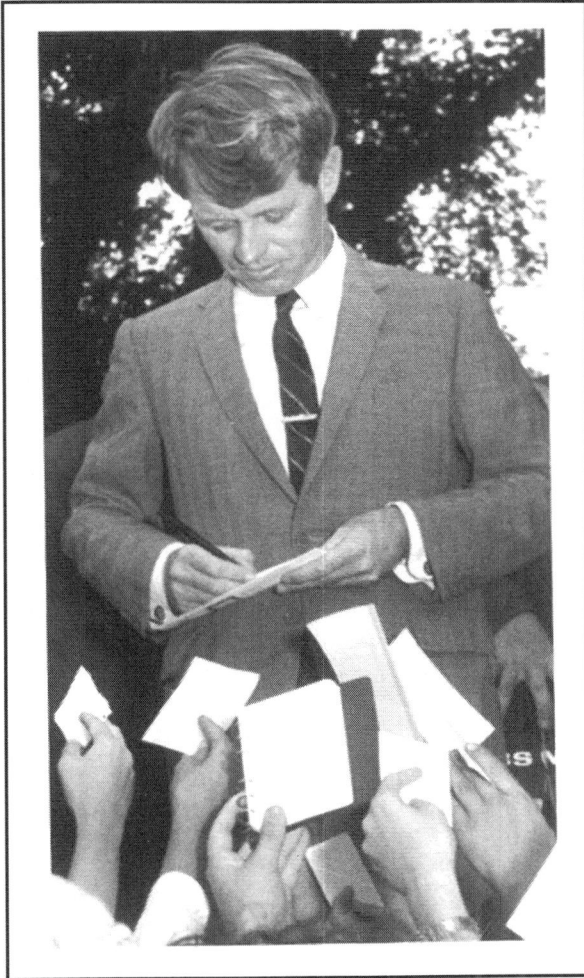

Photo courtesy of Nobles County Minnesota Historical Society

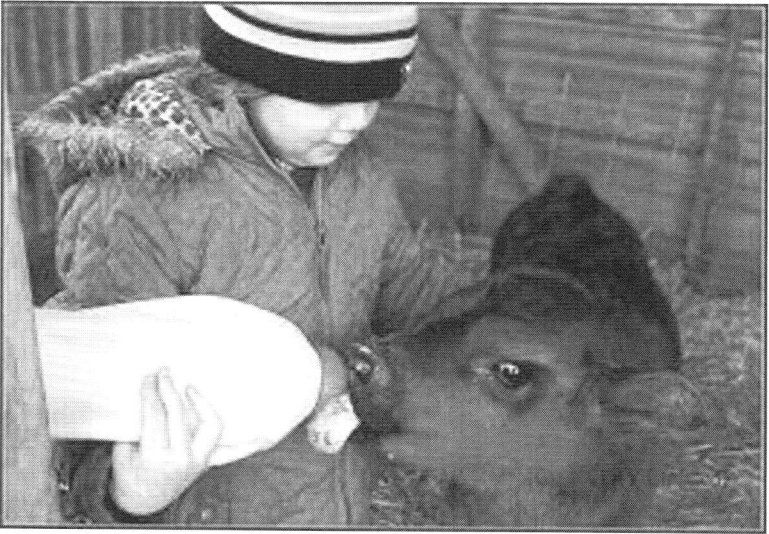

Photo provided by Evelyn Moeller

DEBBIE, THE FAMILY COW
Evelyn Moeller

The calf came to us because its mother had rejected it, the second in a set of twins, shortly after birth. My sister Frances and I were in the barn playing with a litter of kittens that cold spring day when Dad carried the calf into the barn and set it down on a pile of hay. The little thing didn't even try to stand. Still covered with mucous and other birth fluids, it could barely hold its head up. Dad grabbed some rag-towels and began vigorously rubbing the calf down.

Frances and I had already left the kittens and gone to watch. Dad, his big, work-roughened hands gentle on the calf, told us we'd all have to work hard if the calf were to have a chance of survival. Then he handed each of us a towel and told us to keep rubbing the calf to warm it, and to stimulate circulation. Kneeling, we obeyed. Dad left the barn.

We had seen orphaned calves before at our grandparents' farm, but this was the first time Frances and I had been asked to participate in helping one of our own. We took the job very seriously, and as I rubbed the calf from head to tail, Frances spoke to it in a gentle voice. A short while later dad was back, and this time he had our mother with him. He carried a bucket that sloshed with fresh milk from one of our other Guernseys, while mom had a one-gallon glass bottle and oversized rubber nipple. Working as a team, they poured warm milk into the bottle and then stretched the nipple snuggly over the rim. Under our care the calf had perked up a bit. With some help from Mom it struggled to its feet, and stood on wobbly legs.

Holding the bottle out to me, Dad said simply, "Here you go."

Surprised, I took the bottle, feeling the heat of the milk through the glass. I held the bottle out to the calf, then closer, and nudged its nose with the nipple. The calf latched on and began to drink. Mom and Dad smiled as Frances jumped up and down, squealing with delight. Being eighteen months older than my sister, I felt it my duty to behave with more dignity than that, but inside I was every bit as excited.

After that, Frances and I took turns feeding the calf, which we named Debbie because we'd recently seen *Singin' in the Rain* at the movie theater, and had loved it. Debbie the calf did not lack for attention. Soon she was following Frances and me around everywhere we went, bawling for the bottle if she was hungry, but usually just content to be near us. She loved having her ears scratched, and Frances seemed to have the magic touch in that department.

At one month of age we started giving Debbie a mash of milk, grain, and raw eggs to supplement her bottle feedings. She grew quickly, stronger every day. She became acquainted with the other animals on our farm, which, besides the many cats, included Frisco, our dog, and Sugar and Spice, two pygmy goats.

At night she slept in the barn, usually with a few barn kittens curled up on her back and shoulders, enjoying her body heat. On sunny days, when she got tired of following us around, she would explore the pastures, literally kicking up her heels with joy. When she grew big enough we took turns riding on her back. If she got tired of us being on her she would fold first her front legs, sending us lurching forward, clinging to her neck, then her back legs, and lower herself until her belly was on the ground. That was our signal to get off!

When school started that fall, Frances and I returned to our regular routine of getting on the bus at eight in the morning and we wouldn't get home again until nearly four. The first couple of mornings Debbie, by then a hefty 600 pounds, stood at the pasture fence closest to the road and moo-ed sadly as the bus took us away.

The forced separation from us made Debbie seek out other companionship. Though we had a few other Guernseys on our farm, two of which had calves, her best pals became Sugar and Spice, the goats. The three became inseparable. No longer would it be just Debbie waiting for us at the fence when the school bus dropped us off. It was a whole menagerie, half-grown calf and goats, our own welcoming committee.

Eventually Debbie began to lose interest in her human friends. She hung out mostly with Sugar and Spice, who now slept with her in the barn. Maybe the small goats satisfied some maternal instinct in Debbie, who would never experience motherhood herself. As the female half of male/female twins, she'd been born sterile. Being farm kids we knew this, but it had never occurred to us that our parents assumed the bottle calf would be raised for meat. Until one day when Frances and I overheard them talking, and the horrible reality dawned.

Our parents tried to make us understand that feeding an animal the size of Debbie, one that would never produce young or even milk to earn her keep, was impractical. But Frances and I were inconsolable.

God bless our parents! Too kind to break our little hearts, they eventually relented. Debbie grew to be a 1,110-pound pet who, with her goat friends, continued to greet the school bus nearly every day for the next several years.

Evelyn Moeller believes that life on a family farm in Kansas taught her many important lessons, including the value of hard work. She married a city boy, but eventually they took over the farm when her parents retired. They raised four children in the same house she grew up in. Her sister Frances became a large-animal veterinarian.

OL' BILL THE GOAT
Sam Kaderly

In March of 1953, my sister Marie was born, the sixth child in a family of eight. Right from the start she was a fussy baby, with a lot of colic and gastric problems. Soon it was discovered that she was allergic to cow's milk, which is what babies during that time were given if they weren't breast fed.

Shortly thereafter my grandpa showed up with a nanny goat. The task of milking the goat was delegated to the three oldest kids—Nancy, eleven; Eddie, ten; and me, age nine.

Once Marie was started on the goat's milk everything was better in her world.

At first the nanny goat was kept in a pen in the driveway of the haymow. She often escaped, and we had to chase her and catch her before she could be milked. And she did *not* like to be milked. She would kick and stomp and put her feet in the bucket. Two of us had to hold her while one milked, or, if she was in a calm mood, one would hold her and two would milk to get it done faster.

All I can say, looking back on this process, is that it's a good thing that strainers and pasteurization had been invented because they were certainly needed. Anyway, the baby was thriving.

Our grandpa was the kind of guy who thought you should try to make a buck no matter what you were doing. That meant if you had a nanny goat you needed a billy goat, and some time that summer he showed up with one in the back of his 1946 Chevy truck.

The first thing we noticed was that this goat didn't just smell bad—he just plain stunk.

The second thing was that he was big, with a set of fully-curled horns. We quickly learned that he knew how to use them.

We took him to meet his new lady friend. She was not impressed.

Ol' Bill, as he was called, would not stay penned. He soon had the run of the farmstead, terrorizing everyone and everything he saw. He chased all of us kids, the family dog and anyone who arrived in a car. It helped to keep the salesmen at bay, but the rest of the time we just had to keep our eyes, ears and nose open as to where Ol' Bill was.

One day Ol' Bill was in the cow yard eating leftovers out of the bunk when our four-year-old Holstein bull came to get a drink. This bull was very large and very ill-tempered. He also thought he was the king of the farm.

When he saw the goat he let out a bellow that shook the windows in the barn. The goat hopped out of the bunk and turned to stand his ground. The bull lowered his head and charged. The goat took a leap toward the bull, left the ground and hit him square-on, like a sledge hammer. There was a very loud *thunk*, and the bull's eyes rolled back in his head as he dropped like a ton of bricks.

The goat backed up for a second charge, but decided it wasn't needed and calmly went back to eating.

After a few moments the bull came to, staggered to his feet and limped away.

That incident led Ol' Bill to decide he now ruled the cow yard as well. He started charging the cows, and soon cows had bruised udders that developed into mastitis. Dad got a fifty-pound cement block and a chain and tied it around the goat's neck. Everywhere Ol' Bill went he had to drag the block, which slowed him down considerably. This worked really well, and he was put in a pasture downhill from the house.

One day Ol' Bill jumped the fence, leaving him stuck on a very short chain on one side with the cement block on the other. A city person came walking down the road, saw this "poor animal" and decided to set the goat free. The "poor animal" showed his appreciation by chasing his rescuer all the way back up to our farmstead.

Ol' Bill was on the loose again. Dad said we needed to get the block back on him. After a lot of chasing, my brothers and I managed to get him into the barn, but we still couldn't catch him. So we decided to have a little fun. We tied a gunny sack to a piece of twine, and lowered in down from a hay chute. We shook it until it caught the goat's eye, and then when he charged we would yank it back up. He hit the wall with a loud *CRACK!*

Hitting the wall was no deterrent for Ol' Bill. He did it over and over until he broke one of his horns loose from his head.

The loose horn now grew crooked, and shortly after that we had to catch him and saw off the tip so it wouldn't grow into the side of his head. When we were done our mother made us leave our smelly clothes outside and go directly to the bathtub.

Then, in the fall, Grandpa was at the farm like usual, helping with the chores. He was getting the slop ready for the hogs, which consisted of mixing whey and ground oats in an old wooden tank. When finished he would run it out into troughs for the hogs.

I told Grandpa he'd better watch out for Ol' Bill. He just laughed and said he wasn't afraid of a little goat.

Grandpa was bent over the wooden tank, stirring the slop, when the goat approached. Ol' Bill hit him from behind, and Grandpa went headfirst into the tank. When he climbed out, the wad of chew which was usually between his cheek and gum was gone, presumably swallowed. He was madder than a wet hen.

Saying a few choice words that could not be repeated, he headed for the house. A minute later he came back out with Dad's .22 rifle.

The goat took off for the woods with Grandpa in pursuit. It wasn't long before we heard the repeat of the rifle shot.

Ol' Bill was dead.

Never one to waste anything, Grandpa butchered the old billy goat, but the meat turned out to be so bad that Grandma threw it out. Soon our little sister was big enough that she didn't need the nanny goat's milk anymore.

That was end of goats on our farm.

Sam Kaderly grew up on a 360-acre dairy farm in south central Wisconsin, the third of eight children. He and his wife bought their own farm in 1976 and sold it in 1994. Now he enjoys woodworking, beekeeping, making maple syrup and writing about the crazy things he and his siblings did while growing up.

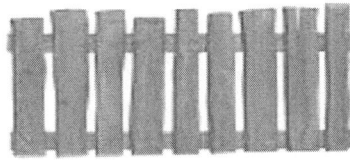

Photo provided by Kathy Erickson

PRETTY AS A PICTURE
Kathy Ericksen

Like many who were born in the early 1900s, my grandfather talked about living in simpler times. My grandmother, who came from Germany, was interested in American gadgets that claimed to make life easier. He said they were unnecessary, because they gave the wife more to clean.

"Let's just keep things simple," was Grandpa's motto. He didn't seem to consider that a few gadgets could have simplified my grandmother's life, and as usual, things went his way.

At that time, dairies kept things simple too. People came in to purchase their items. Then, as a marketing tool, the dairies began to deliver milk to their customers. In addition, they carried butter, half and half, sour cream, various kinds of cheese, cottage cheese, and other items kept readily available. These home deliveries helped to get products into the hands of customers and made things simpler for the public.

If you lived in the 1940s you may recall having or seeing milk boxes. These were insulated metal boxes that carried the names of the dairies. They sat in suitable spots on front porches or steps for the deliveryman's convenience. The boxes made purchasing products so much simpler and kept milk from freezing in the winter or becoming too warm in the summer. Residents possessing milk boxes had a standard delivery order and date. They called in orders, and the deliveryman would arrive at the house in his milk truck at the scheduled time.

It was a nice way to purchase items without leaving home, rather like ordering off the Internet today.

As a young woman in the early 1940s, my mother, Florence Yahn Meise, and her friends enjoyed playing around with their cameras. It was inexpensive entertainment, and Mom filled her black photo album with pictures of herself and her friends enjoying the pleasant outdoor weather. As a child, I liked to pore over those pictures of my young, pretty mother.

Mom was posing on the porch steps of her parents' home one warm, sunny day in Watertown, Wisconsin, when her friend Lois snapped her picture. Mom was attired in a white scooped-neck peasant blouse with a bright floral skirt and white sandal heels. She was an attractive young woman with dark, curly hair. She didn't know it then, but that picture was destined to bring an unusual opportunity to her door.

Many pictures later, when the roll of film was completed, Mom dropped it off at the local drug store to have it developed. Privacy laws that we have these days definitely weren't in effect at that time, and more than one person in town got a look at the pictures before Mom picked them up.

A few days passed, when a well-dressed man rang the doorbell and asked for Florence. Surprised, Mom told him that she was Florence. He said he worked for Brinkman's Dairy and they were interested in hiring her to be a model for their company.

Unbeknownst to Mom, the picture of her posing on her home's porch steps had included their local dairy's milk box, and since the picture was quite appealing, the owner of Brinkman's Dairy was enthused about using it for their ads. The well-dressed man was carrying a briefcase, and in it was contract for her to sign that very day!

Unfortunately, Mom had not yet reached the age of 21, so she would have to check with her father before signing anything. German fathers were quite protective in those days, and my grandfather was not excited about his daughter being used in advertising strategies. He was accustomed to having things his own way, so when she approached him with the man's request, a firm NO was his response.

This quickly ended Mom's brief dreams of a modeling career.

I loved seeing that picture as a child, and every time I did, I would again question Mom about it, and she would retell the milk box picture story. I was always so proud of my beautiful mother, and I dreamed of what it would have been like if her picture had been on the cover of *Brinkman's Dairy* magazines! A simple "yes" from my grandfather could have made all the difference.

Kathy Meise Ericksen grew up in Watertown, Wisconsin. As a Pastor's wife, she was active in her husband's ministry in congregations in Kansas, Nebraska, and Iowa. She writes skits for various occasions, loves to sing, and actively promotes the mission of Camp Okoboji in the Iowa Great Lakes Region. She enjoyed working in the bank, but most of all, loves her role as wife, mother, and grandmother. They are presently retired in Hartley, Iowa.

Photo provided by Betty Taylor

Photo provided by Carmen Folkestad

BAD HAIR DAYS
Carmen Folkestad

A lot of people claim to like naturally curly hair. They call it "charming," and "bouncy." They spend a lot of money on perms, hoping to get just the look they want. They express envy for those who come by it naturally. But as the owner of naturally curly hair, I could tell them a thing or two.

As a preschooler, my wild, strawberry-blonde hair tangled easily, and my mother tried everything from expensive store-bought conditioners to homemade concoctions her friends recommended to get it to relax enough to run a brush through. One recipe I remember in particular as being a mayonnaise-and-ginger ale mix that didn't relax my curls but caused the dog to follow me around the yard with his tongue hanging out and nose twitching.

By the time I started kindergarten, Mom sort of gave up and just kept my hair pulled back into a ponytail with a rubber band. This was okay to a point, but when the rubber bands broke my hair would spring free like one of those crazy explosive party-favors. The fact that I was a tomboy made it worse. There was many a day that I came home from school with the hem of my skirt torn from climbing the playground equipment and my hair a mass of tangles around my head.

Then, in the summer after fourth grade, I came home after a hot afternoon of playing in a newly-discovered empty lot with some friends, with my hair so full of cockleburs that Mom had no choice but to cut it off short. I think we both felt a sense of relief. Short hair was so much easier to take care of, and mercifully didn't tangle.

My hair stayed short until junior high, when adolescent vanity got the best of me and I insisted on letting it grow to shoulder length. It was still hard to manage, but the task no longer fell to my mother. Now it was my responsibility to control that wild mass.

Enter Dippity-Do. It came in a pink jar, and in the 1960s it was the miracle product I'd been looking for. After each shampoo I would towel-dry my hair, then dip my fingertips into the jar of Dippity-Do, rub my palms together and then run my hands over and through my damp hair. Next I would roll my hair up into three-inch pink plastic rollers, held in place by bobby pins. After sitting with my mom's cap-style hair dryer on my head for thirty minutes or so, I would remove the rollers and carefully brush out my hair. It was smooth, lovely, and the fly-aways were under control. For the most part.

Summers were still difficult because of the high humidity in southern Minnesota. Humidity worked against my hair. I had to increase the usage of my miracle gel, and since no one else in the family used it, I was expected to pay for it myself from my babysitting money. That was okay. I considered the expense well worth it.

Things worked out well. The pink gel did its job. I began to bravely experiment with different hairstyles. One of my favorites was an up-do that I saved for special occasions because it was way too sophisticated for every day.

One of those special occasions came in the form of the homecoming dance my junior year. I'd been invited to the dance by Bobby Bachman, a senior. I was beyond thrilled and prepared for the dance with special care. We were having a particularly late, hot summer, so the dress I sewed for the dance was sleeveless, and stopped two inches above my knees—pretty bold for those days.

On the day of the dance the temperature rose to ninety-five degrees, and the humidity level was out of this world. I worried about keeping my hair in place, so doubled up on the Dippity-Do. I may even have tripled-up on it. A wide headband added a finishing touch. When I was done my hair looked like a pale strawberry helmet on my head, but by golly every hair stayed in place.

Bobby came to the house, pinned a corsage to my dress and my mother took pictures with her Polaroid. I felt beautiful.

The dance was held in the gym. Windows had been opened to provide a breeze, but it was inadequate, and there was no air conditioning. As more excited couples arrived, the temperature in the gym climbed and it became almost unbearably stuffy.

A small local band began to play on the makeshift stage. We danced.

At first the band played the popular songs of the day—"Mony Mony" by Tommy James and the Shondells; "Help Me, Rhonda" by the Beach Boys, and others. But kids began to collapse. Two girls fainted and had to be taken outside. Others left on their own accord, sneaking out the side doors for some much needed fresh air.

Even the streamers hanging from the rafters seemed to droop.

The band switched to songs that weren't so physically demanding. Bobby and I danced to "Unchained Melody" by the Righteous Brothers.

Then I noticed Bobby was looking at me sort of funny. At first I thought he was just so entranced by my beauty. But... he didn't look entranced. He looked puzzled. Then a little alarmed.

Something dripped in my eye. Smiling, embarrassed to be caught sweating but sure he'd understand considering the heat, I lifted a dainty hand to touch my forehead. I'd have to excuse myself to the girls' bathroom soon and blot my face with some paper towels. But instead of touching some ladylike perspiration, my fingers encountered something thicker. And sticky.

Bobby fumbled in his pocket and handed me a clean white handkerchief. I touched it to my brow. I realized then that the Dippity-Do had succumbed to the atmosphere in the gym and was melting. It was running down my scalp and temples, soaking my headband and dragging loose, damp strands of hair with it.

"Uh, excuse me," I mumbled. Holding Bobby's handkerchief to my eyebrows, I bolted from the dance floor and to the girls' bathroom.

The bedraggled reflection that peered back at me from the mirror was only one of many. There were other girls crammed into that small space as well.

My melted hair gel had streaked its way downward through my makeup. My hair flopped to one side, looking as though the strawberry had been nipping at some spiked punch. But at least my hair hadn't run black rivers down my face as Sadie Jesperson's had. She'd dyed her hair just that morning, thinking black over her lovely natural brown would look "funky." What she looked like was one of the ghouls from a particularly scary movie that had been making the rounds lately. And poor Marilyn Gannon. She'd applied heavy false eyelashes for the dance. Sobbing, she told us that her date had been snickering for nearly half an hour before she finally figured out that one of the eyelashes had long ago been released by an excess of perspiration and was resting on her cheek.

With a handful of wet paper towels I cleaned the gel from my face. Dry paper towels helped soak up the excess that was still in my hair. My headband went into the trash. Someone gave me a rubber band, and I pulled my hair back into a ponytail.

When we emerged from the bathroom the gym was nearly empty. Even the band was gone. Once the heat had become unbearable, wiser minds had prevailed and the festivities were in the process of being moved outside.

Bobby was kind when I explained about the hair gel. At least he hadn't laughed at me and let me continue on, oblivious to what was going on, as Marilyn's date had. We danced a little more, in the more comfortable night air, and later he drove me home and kissed me good-night.

But he didn't ask me out again. And a couple of weeks later I had my hair trimmed into a flattering "pixie" cut that a model named Twiggy had made popular.

Vanity aside, I've found it's a style that has continued to work well for me over the years.

After high school **Carmen Folkestad** left the humidity-prone region of Minnesota for the University of Arizona in Tucson, where, as the saying goes, "It's a dry heat." After earning a nursing degree she realized she hated the sight of blood, went to cosmetology school and learned to cut hair. She still keeps hers short.

THE BARNYARD STADIUM
Thomas D. Phillips

It all began with the after-chores "nothing to do, no one to play with" grousing of a young boy growing up on a farm a mile or so away from the nearest neighbors. My mother, a terrific baseball fan, got tired of hearing it, found a used ball and glove and showed me how to throw the ball on the roof of a small shed and catch it as it rolled back down.

Soon the low granary did not present enough of a challenge, so I took my game to the barn, a much taller building with a steep gable. There, the ball came off much faster—except for those times when I threw it too hard and it rolled over the top. Then I had to waste precious minutes trying to find it in the woodpile on the other side.

Eventually, as my fascination with the game grew, the farm itself—the cinder driveway and surrounding grain bins—became, in my mind, a major league ballpark. The famous "Green Monster" left field wall at Fenway Park was really a two-strand barbed wire fence beyond which the family's milk cow grazed

49

placidly in the sun. Toward right field, the chicken coop was about where a first base dugout would be. Down the third base line, grandstands were formed by the barn, a small workshop and one or two parked tractors. Thousands of people sat in those stands—well, really, my dog Smokey and one or two stray cats—all transfixed as I came to bat with the bases loaded and two outs in the bottom of the ninth.

The pasture fence and a long Quonset hut formed stadium walls that I tried to clear by hitting rocks with a wooden stick. With Mom's intervention my dad tolerated—just barely—a cracked windshield and a several dents in the sides of two tin sheds.

Later, I outlined a strike zone with chalk on the side of the barn and spent countless hours pitching imaginary games with an old tennis ball. Eventually I borrowed a roll of black tape and marked the strike zone into quadrants: high inside, high outside, low inside, and low outside.

Any miss from the square I was throwing at constituted a hit for the other team. The farther the miss, the longer the hit.

Fortunately for me, my parents smiled at the good-natured jests of the neighbors who saw my strike zone while driving past and commented that my artwork messed up the appearance of an otherwise nice-looking farm building.

When I was twelve, I pitched a perfect game against that barn. I was determined not to fudge or let up, even though in the ninth inning I fell behind 3-0 in the count to the leadoff hitter. Luckily, the next three pitches were all in the low outside box, just where they were intended to be. Much to my mother's bemusement I walked around the house smiling and quite cocky. But eventually that got to be too much, and for the next several days I was given extra chores.

In later years I have on occasion driven past that long-since abandoned farmstead. Each time, visions of the perfect game and that grand slam homerun in the bottom of the ninth come flooding back as vividly as if they happened yesterday. In my mind's eye the stadium still exists, far surpassing the magic of any major league ballpark.

Tom Phillips grew up on a farm near Lincoln, Nebraska. After thirty-six years in the military, during which he led a unit through a terrorist episode, served in Desert Storm, and led some of the first American troops into Sarajevo, he worked as a university administrator before beginning a full time career writing about Americana, military history, and baseball.

Photo courtesy of National Oceanic and Atmospheric Administration/Department of Commerce.

More than 900 women were employed by the Weather Bureau as atmospheric observers and forecasters, filling the positions of men during World War II.

MOM, THE WEATHERMAN
Verla Klaessy

W e crouch in front of the TV set daily to watch the weather forecast. It hardly matters if a man or woman is the forecaster. Preceding this hourly report, there has been a great amount of analysis, drawing of isobars and isotherms, plotting maps and turning it into a unique account of momentary weather patterns.

However, in early 1942 in Spencer, Iowa, we didn't have a radio station, and very few women had anything to do with weather reporting.

Mom Klaessy's oldest son, Don, had been the local weather observer. But a war was on, and Don Klaessy had gone off to serve in the Army Air Force. Many people, including pilots at the small local airport, depended on daily weather reports. Reports from Spencer, Iowa were combined with observations across the state. These were added to other states' forecasts and became the national weather announcements.

Mom Klaessy took over the task. A box in her kitchen held a supply of large red balloons. They were about two feet in

53

diameter, and would be inflated with hydrogen, which was kept in a cylinder in the garage. A weight fastened to a balloon indicated that proper inflation had been reached when the balloon lifted off the table.

Mom would inflate a balloon at about eight each morning and release it in the front yard. She observed the balloon for wind direction and counted the seconds until it was out of sight in the clouds. The count revealed the height of the clouds.

Then she would read the thermometers. In a small slatted enclosure in a shady spot in the garden, she kept both a wet-bulb and a dry-bulb thermometer. They had to be a in shady spot for correct air temperature. She first took a reading of the dry-bulb thermometer, then covered the other bulb with a wet cloth and whirled it about for a few minutes. As the water evaporated from the wet cloth the thermometer cooled. The reading depended on the amount of moisture in the air. The difference between the temperatures of the two thermometers measured the moisture, hence humidity was calculated.

Her other weather instrument was a barometer fastened to paper on a cylinder. An attached pen would show a line of barometric pressure to add to her report. The sum total of all this vital information was given every day by telephone to someone at the local airport who in turn relayed it to the U.S. Weather Department.

At five P.M., she sent up another balloon, checked and compared the temperatures, read the barometric pressure, and again called in the report.

One day the younger boys were playing catch with a balloon filled with hydrogen. One of them slid his foot on the rug, causing static electricity resulting in a spark. There was an immediate explosion that blew out a bedroom window and singed his eyebrows.

Soon thereafter, helium, which was non-explosive, was used to fill the balloons.

In the late 1940s the development of electronic computers made calculations quickly and the number of weather stations and frequency of observations increased.

During World War II, pilots flying over Japan made a startling discovery. Winds at certain high altitudes were extremely strong. After the war, meteorologists studied those winds, which became known as the jet stream. Now close attention is paid to the location, strength and movement of these jet streams in all forecasting.

Late in 1942, a radio station was erected in Spencer, Iowa, and Signed (Sig′·nid) Klassey's task was taken over by their staff. She was a terrific homemaker and mother with no formal training in weather reporting. This was her contribution to the war effort. Her reward—$8.00 a week to help buy the groceries and a pride in a job well done.

Verla Klaessy grew up on a farm in Clay County. With her parents she lived through the depression days of the 1930s. she was married to Earl Klaessy for 65 years making their home with their two children Kim and James in Spencer, Iowa.

IT HAPPENED IN SECOND GRADE
Victoria Lindsay

On the last day of school in 1954, we flew through the exits. "School's out! School's out! Teacher let the fools out!" some of the older children chanted.

During the year I had saved my nickels and dimes so I could indulge in the sights, sounds and flavors of summer: The carousel at the county fair. Dips in Silver Lake. Watermelon, fresh from the field. And sweet corn! I could hardly wait. And yet...I stepped into this summer with a last, backward glance at the school door.

That school year, second grade, had begun with a beautiful, young teacher, Miss Maschoff. She had short, dark hair and brown eyes. I thought she looked exotic. I admired her clothes... even her umbrella, with its floral pattern. It was unique. Special.

However, it was what Miss Maschoff *did* that really rocked my world. First, she asked me to assist my classmate, Sylvia. My mission: Help Sylvia learn her spelling words. I was to say the words and have her spell them orally. After that, Sylvia was to correctly write each word she had misspelled on the recent written test. *Ten times.*

As Miss Maschoff picked up Sylvia's paper, an unfamiliar expression played on her face. She had a smile *and* a frown. She glanced at me. "Vicki, did you write this?" she asked.

How had she known? I had felt sorry for Sylvia. She had way too many words for one little girl, so I had helped her out. She'd written some, and I'd written some. I didn't lose my tutoring job, but I didn't write Sylvia's words for her again.

Then, one morning, a loud, BANG shattered the school's silence. The sound had come from somewhere down the hall. A classmate, Wanda, ran screaming from the room. Wanda was always quick to laugh or cry, but I wasn't frightened. There were no hunters in my family, so the sound had meant nothing to me. Besides, Miss Maschoff was calm.

In small town Wisconsin, we had no security at the entrances to our school. No one even thought to lock a school door back then. When Miss Maschoff left the room to check on Wanda, we students just sat there, wondering what was going on. A few even went to the door to peek out, but when Miss Maschoff returned, we resumed our work.

A few minutes later the recess bell rang, and out in the hallway we gathered around the older students who were eager to fill us in. They said there was blood on the ceiling of their classroom. Wanda's brother, Daryl, had brought something to school. That "something" had exploded and had blown off *two* of Daryl's fingers. Weeks passed before I got up the nerve to look at

Daryl's hand. Sure enough, one finger was missing, along with part of another.

I learned so much in second grade! One thing I discovered was that *some teachers hug.* Miss Maschoff was a hugger. At home I was told only to do my best. That was the end of it. I heard no praise for a report card bursting with A's, and there were no hugs. Other children told of getting a dollar for each A on a report card. I didn't. The money wasn't important to me, but I truly did long for those hugs. An arm across my shoulders along with a, "Good job!" was indescribably wonderful. Miss Maschoff was generous with her praise.

Measles ruined my bid for perfect attendance that year. Then, along came the polio scare, which turned personal when a classmate, Stephen, caught it. Stephen was one of the two boys in our small class, and he had dark hair like Miss Maschoff. Stephen disappeared from school for a full year while he rehabbed in Milwaukee.

Because of what had happened to Stephen, we second graders were told we each needed to get a shot. So, on my birthday, I dressed up in my new red poodle skirt for the trek to the doctor's office.

There I was weighed, then given the shot—*not* in the arm. I took note of the name: gamma globulin.

After lunch on that same day I went to school. A chubby girl in our class had brought a pillow to sit on. She'd received *two* shots. I didn't yet know the meaning of the words *drama queen.*

I just thought she was silly. Wasn't she glad she wouldn't get polio? The shot guaranteed that, right?

On any given weekend, the best treat was a sleepover at Grandma Robinson's house. It was only a few blocks away from my home, yet it seemed like a different world. Grandma was a hugger *and* a kisser. When I stayed there I shared a double bed with Aunt Babe.

Early one morning, not long after the vaccination, I awoke at Grandma's and, when I tried to turn over, found I couldn't move. Frightened, I lay there thinking, *What happened? I'm paralyzed. How can I have polio?*

My parents drove up to retrieve me, and a doctor was called to our home. My head felt like it was filled with rocks. I couldn't even raise it from my pillow. But it wasn't polio. A few days later we were told I had scarlet fever... the only case in Wisconsin.

I don't recall how many weeks I lay in my small second floor bedroom. My mom asked what kinds of fruit I would like to eat, then she went downtown and bought it, fresh. I felt pampered. Except for the sweet, juicy strawberries my father grew in the summer, we usually had canned fruit

Of course, other children were kept away from me, so I was surprised when I was told, one afternoon, that I had a visitor. Entered Miss Maschoff, wearing her signature smile. She'd brought me a purple hyacinth, its pot wrapped in light green foil and decorated with a lilac bow.

Years later, I don't remember what Miss Maschoff said, but I can still see her smile and the purple hyacinth.

As the school year ended, I thought of all that had happened. And I knew that I wanted to be a teacher, just like Miss Maschoff. She had made me realize that I was smart enough. I knew that I, too, could give good hugs.

Miss Maschoff told us she was going to move away during the summer. She was getting married, and would have a new name after her June wedding. She would be Mrs. Floor. *Mrs. Floor,* I thought. *Why would she want that name?*

Yes, I became a teacher. Thank-you, Miss Maschoff... I mean *Mrs. Floor,* wherever you are.

Victoria Lindsay grew up in Portage, Wisconsin and began her teaching career there. She has created innovative education programs for all ages and ability levels in California, Wisconsin and Missouri. She credits her small town community, her best teachers and her parents for their emphasis on excellence, kindness and participation. Currently living in northern Wisconsin, she is a poet, playwright, actor, storyteller, professional clown emeritus, writer of fiction and non-fiction... a creative explorer. She has two grandchildren and delights in traveling with her husband, Joe.

BEST FRIENDS

Carolyn Rohrbaugh

I had several best friends when I grew up. Squeaky, my dog, was a best friend who came to our house with a bullet wound in his leg. I loved him more than any pet I have ever had. We wrote the ABCs and our names with chalk on the sidewalk—at least I thought he could write. He waited for me to come home from school and he remained at my side, except when we played cowboys and Indians when he would disappear. He couldn't bark, just squeaked in such a way that even today I can still hear him in my thoughts. And he always listened to my problems.

My best girlfriend was Kary, who lived two houses down. We played house in our playhouse, rocked our dolls, and dressed up in hand-me down dresses from the neighbor's grown children. We dreamed about boyfriends and walked to school together. We sat on her front porch and talked about the things we would do when we grew up. She was quiet, kind and gentle, while I, on the other hand, had a bit of the tomboy in me.

Each morning I flew off our porch, doing cartwheels until I reached her house. Our neighbor, Charlie Williams, made stilts for us. I was the only one who mastered walking on them. I would climb a tree to see the whole neighborhood and try to touch the sky. When I learned to ride a bicycle I rode as fast as I could, which meant I often tipped over and ended up with bruised and skinned elbows and knees.

Mike and Gerald were my age and also lived in the neighborhood. They were my best boy friends—I mean *boys* who were my *friends*. When we played cowboys and Indians I would dress up in the cowgirl outfit I'd received for Christmas, and Mike and Gerald would bring their guns and holsters. That's when Squeaky would disappear.

Mike's dad, Bob, took care of the city dump, a large area where everyone took their garbage. Bob used a tractor to push the garbage into piles and then over an embankment to make room for more.

Mike, Gerald and I sometimes went to the dump to club rats and dig for treasures. On one of our adventures we found a coffee can filled with old tobacco pipes. Mike had an idea. His family raised rabbits and fed them ground alfalfa. "We'll pack alfalfa into the pipes and smoke them," he stated. "Mom is gone, let's try it now."

We ran as fast as we could to his house, packed the pipes with ground alfalfa and began to puff. I can't tell you how bad it tasted. I credit that experience with never smoking anything again.

Bob changed jobs and drove a rendering truck. Mike would ride with him to the rendering plant, and one day he asked me to ride along. As Bob unloaded the dead animals from the truck, Mike and I climbed on mountains of dead animals. Mike wanted to see what would happen if he stabbed a bloated cow with his pocket knife, but, thankfully, Bob called and said he was ready to leave.

One day as Squeaky and I were walking to Gerald's house, I spotted Gerald holding his BB gun. I asked if it was loaded. When he said "yes," I didn't believe him. So I asked a second time if the gun was really loaded. Gerald looked at me and said, "If you don't believe me, put your tongue over the end and I'll pull the trigger."

I don't know if it was innocence or bliss, but I put my tongue over the end of the barrel and Gerald pulled the trigger.

I ran home faster than Squeaky. My mouth was bleeding but I wouldn't 'fess up to putting my tongue over the end of that BB gun. Instead, I told Mother that Gerald hit me.

The BB remained in my tongue, and eventually I told mother the truth. When I was eight I had my tonsils out, and the doctor took the BB out of my tongue at the same time.

Growing up is filled with experiences. Some we would do again and others we wouldn't dream of doing. But we have the memories, and friends to cherish forever.

Carolyn Rohrbaugh has lived in Sutherland, Iowa, her entire life. She says, "Growing up in the forties and fifties was an experience never again to be duplicated. It was truly a time of lazy, hazy, crazy days of summer, innocence and freedom."

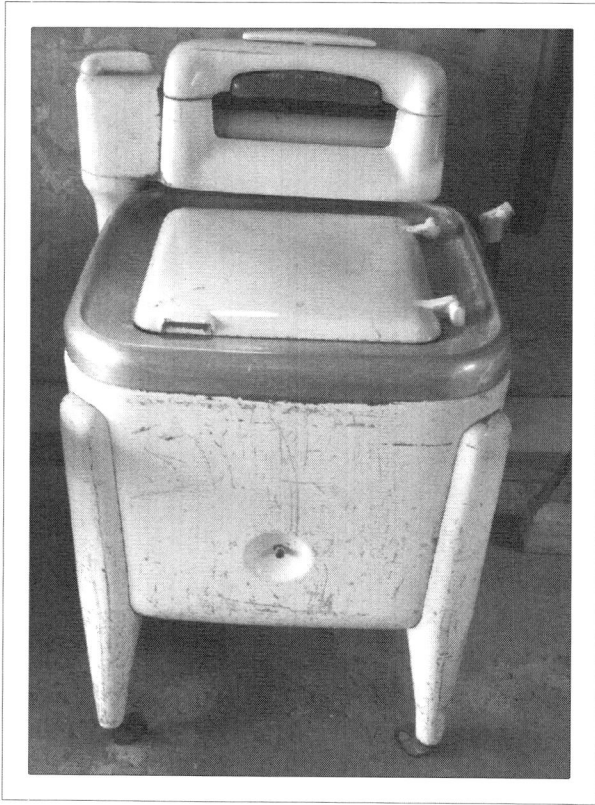

VARMINTS IN THIS OLD HOUSE
Marie Wells

Moving back to the old Wells' family home was a bittersweet experience in 1977. We had previously lived in the house, but three years earlier had moved to a county seat town to take advantage of job opportunities there.

My younger daughter had just graduated from high school. The day after we moved, in August, she was off to college. I was happy to be back among my friends but I had never lived alone before and wasn't looking forward to it. This old house was indeed old, having been built in 1880 and purchased by my husband's grandfather in 1899. At times it creaked and groaned, and when a train passed nearby it shuddered. Sometimes it felt spooky.

Soon after I'd moved in, varmints never before seen began arriving. Upon opening the basement door one Saturday, a beady-eyed squirrel stared back up at me. I slammed the door in its face. How could it have gotten in? I discovered an eight-inch round opening in the side of the brick chimney, running down through the basement. I found the cover and plugged the hole. No more squirrels.

A few months later, one night as I was reading a book, I heard what sounded like a baby crying in the stairwell. Armed with a plastic bat and flashlight, I cautiously approached the staircase. Two-thirds of the way up the stairwell there was a small window above the outdoor porch room. The storm window had four sections; an upper section had loosened and fallen out. A baby raccoon had climbed into the missing area, fallen to the bottom and was crying for help. When I tapped on the inside window with the bat, he climbed up the window frame, out of the hole and onto the porch roof. After turning on the outside light, I saw a mother raccoon and three babies on the roof. The next day I retrieved the unbroken glass, put up my ladder, climbed on the porch roof and caulked the glass back into place.

After attending a movie with a friend one Saturday night, I arrived home to find my cat, Ming, frantically leaping at a bat that was swooping about near the ceiling. Fearing the bat was rabid, I shut Ming in another room. Meantime, the bat had flown up the open staircase. My bedroom was upstairs! No way was I going to sleep up there, or even downstairs. Recalling that I had seen a light on at my friend Jackie's house, I called and asked if I could sleep on her couch. She consented.

After church on Sunday, I asked my friend Roberta to come home with me for some bat-hunting. Like two detectives, we looked high and low but found no bat. I had seen a square hole surrounding an old soil pipe in the upstairs bathroom, leaving four open areas at the corners. Could the bat have escaped into the attic? I sawed out a square of plywood a bit bigger than the hole, drew a circle on it the size of the soil pipe, cut the square in two and sawed out the circle. Fitting the pieces around the soil pipe, I secured them in place with screws. The bat wasn't seen again, but there was an obnoxious odor emanating from the attic for several days.

While sitting in my recliner one day, I noticed something small and black zipping around the perimeter of my living room. It wasn't a mouse. It was too big, too black and had too short of a tail for a mouse. Suddenly it charged across the room, up onto my chair and tried to crawl into my pocket. Never before had I moved so fast!

For that brief moment, though, I had seen its pointed snout. Looking for a similar picture in the encyclopedia, I learned that it was a European shrew, a small rodent with a voracious appetite, and its favorite food was mice. I'd had an influx of mice that fall. Maybe that's what had attracted the shrew to my house.

Roberta was horrified later to learn that I was feeding the shrew table scraps to supplement its mouse diet. But the mice had magically disappeared, and that was good enough for me. When winter came, however, it was time for my annual trip to stay with daughter Marilyn. Without the extra food and water I'd been leaving, the shrew most likely left for better quarters.

For a year after Ming died I was catless. One day a big gray and white striped cat appeared outside of my screened patio door. As I watched, he lifted one huge paw and drew it down through the nylon screen, leaving a twelve-inch rip. After calmly walking through the hole, he sat himself down on the carpet as if he owned the place. It was clear that he'd been someone's house cat. Perhaps they had moved and left him behind. I decided to keep him, and called him simply Cat.

Cat was a friendly fellow, living in and out of the house days and outside at night. One night when it was pouring rain, I shut him in the utility room. Evidently he didn't like being confined, as he tore down the curtain on the outside door. A day later he was gone. But the rip in the screen remained.

My son-in-law, Scott, whom I sometimes call Mr. Fixit, and my daughter Cheri offered to replace the screen. They didn't find the time immediately, and the following Sunday, while reading the Sunday paper, I saw a grey creature scuttle past my chair. It was about a foot long and five inches high. It waddled the length of my nineteen-foot dining room and scooted under the studio couch at the other end. I wasn't about to flush it out on my own. I needed help, but whom? I finally decided to call our fire chief, Jerry Abbas, who arrived a short while later with his wife Starr and their two kids. Jerry barricaded his family and me in the kitchen behind a long couch cushion. He then moved the couch and herded the beast out through the patio door, where he killed it. He told us it was a woodchuck, which was probably rabid or it wouldn't have come into the house. It had come in through the slit in the patio screen door.

About three years ago I acquired my current cat from a family that was moving away. He was named Peanut, which seemed an unlikely moniker for a sixteen-pound feline. But Peanut was furry and purry and very affectionate. Apparently he is also a varmint deterrent. There have been no more squirrels, no more raccoons, no bats, or shrews, or mice, or strange cats or woodchucks invading. There is no one here but Peanut and me.

Aah! There is peace at last in this old house!

Marie Wells has lived in "this old house" in the small town of Marathon (pop. 250) for over 50 years. When the house was young, Marathon was a bustling town of over 600 people and had over 30 businesses. As transportation improved, area residents ventured farther away to shop for life's necessities. Businesses closed and populations dwindled. But it is still a great place to live!

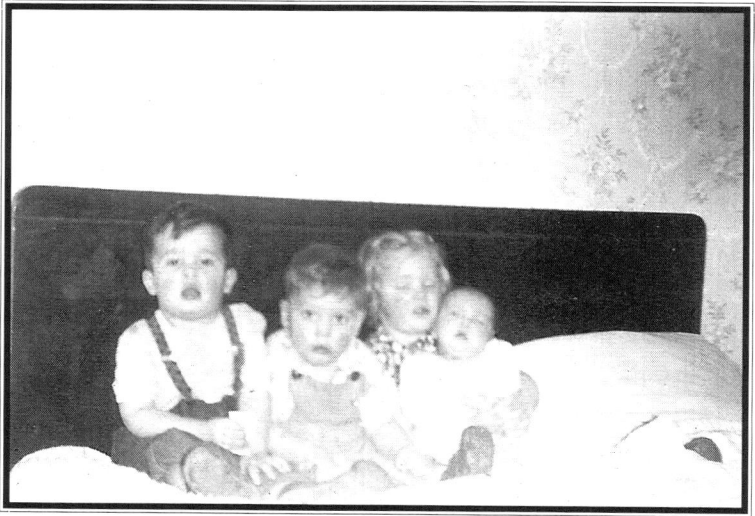

Photo provided by Roger Brockshus

THE FAMILY DOCTOR
Judith Houska

Recently I had to select a new, younger doctor at my medical clinic because my doctor of many decades had retired. Being retirement age myself, I understood my doctor's wish to start taking it easy in his life and to travel and visit grandkids, but I knew I'd miss him.

The receptionist at the office showed me a list of five doctors, both men and women, who had recently come to the clinic. Each brief profile included a small photograph. I might as well have gone "eeny-meeny-miney-moe" for all the interest I took in any of them. Finally I told her I didn't care, and let the clinic choose for me.

My next appointment, a follow-up to a bronchial infection I'd had a couple of months earlier, was with one of the men doctors. After waiting for only a few minutes, I was taken to his office by a nurse. The doctor, one of the men, asked me a few questions about my cough as he scrolled through what I assumed was my file on the laptop he brought into the room with him. Then he turned away from the laptop, turned his chair to face me, and ... well, at least he made the attempt. He listened to my lungs with his stethoscope, and looked into my eyes when he asked how I was feeling and if I'd had any side effects from the course of antibiotics I'd been on. But there was, at the same time, something impersonal about the visit. He didn't quite glance at his watch as I spoke, but I still felt rushed, and when I left the clinic a few minutes later I couldn't help thinking how this visit had been different from those I'd experienced as a child.

Our family doctor when I'd been growing up in South Dakota was named Dr. Mooney. I never even knew his first name, but I knew his kindly manner, and the gentle way he had when he made a house call. Back then, that's what doctors did.

As one of six children, our family knew its share of mishaps. My brother Albert, the oldest, broke his leg jumping from the hayloft when he was eight. I was four, but I clearly remember our mother's relief when Dr. Mooney's big, dusty-black car pulled up in front of our country house. Albert had been carried into the house and made as comfortable on the front room davenport, but he was clearly in pain. From the far side of the room, I watched as Dr. Mooney sat on the straight backed chair Mother had provided for him. I stayed very quiet, because I was afraid if I made a peep Mother would notice I was there and send me out. I didn't want to leave. I was very curious about what was going to happen to Albert. Would they cut his leg off? When my dolls leg got broken, I'd tried to glue it back on with flour paste, but the paste hadn't held and after that I had a doll with just one leg. Would that happen to Albert?

But Dr. Mooney spoke soothingly as he gave Albert a sip of something from a bottle, then gently pulled his trousers off and examined the injury. Fortunately, he told my parents, it wasn't a bad break and Albert would not have to go to the hospital. I don't remember a lot of what was done next, but Albert ended up with a plaster cast on the lower part of his leg, and didn't have to do chores for over a month.

Dr. Mooney came to our house other times as well. Baby sister June was born in the hospital in Spearfish, but she was small and colicky, and Dr. Mooney made many visits to check on her, sometimes in the middle of the night. June outgrew the colic, and by two years of age she was a big, strong girl who looked like she hadn't been sick a day in her life.

Not all of the illnesses I witnessed had such a good outcome. One of our hired hands, an aloof man I knew only as Bernard, scraped his shoulder on some rusted barbed wire, fell sick within a couple of days and was dead by the end of the week. My parents had wanted to take him to the hospital but he refused. It might not have helped him anyway.

When I was nine I contracted whooping cough. We'd heard talk of a vaccine for the disease, but the vaccine was not yet readily available. I remained quarantined from the rest of the family, sequestered in a room that had been stripped bare of everything other than my bed. Mother brought my meals on a tray while wearing a cotton mask over her mouth that Dr.

Mooney had given her. She also wore thick rubber gloves, and kept them on while giving me sponge baths and stripping the sheets to be washed in a separate tub far from the house.

And Dr. Mooney visited me in my sterile little room nearly every day. He didn't wear a mask. When my mother asked him, I heard him tell her he'd already been exposed to so many different illnesses that he figured he was pretty much immune to them all. After the first visit, when I had been too miserable to do much more than whimper, he often brought little gifts for me. Once it was a coloring book and eight crayons. Another time he brought me a box of paper dolls. These thoughtful gifts allowed me to entertain myself for the many hours I would be alone in my room.

As my fever and cough lessened and I began to feel better, Dr. Mooney sometimes stayed with me for as long as an hour, cheerfully playing paper dolls as though it were the most natural thing in the world for a silver-haired man to be doing. I thought he was old, wise, and the kindest man I would ever know.

That latter part was probably true, but many years later, when I attended Dr. Mooney's funeral, I realized that during that time when I'd had whooping cough he was only in his mid-forties. But as a child, I'd thought him ancient.

No doctor into my adulthood could ever compare to Dr. Mooney. Gone were house calls. Visits to the medical clinic were the only way you saw your family doctor, unless you were in the hospital.

I can't really wish to go back to those times, though. When I was in grade school two of my best friends died from the measles, and another was crippled by polio. Maybe that's the trade-off we've made. Medicine has improved, vaccines are widely available to most people in the United States, and we live longer. But our doctors are busier and can no longer take the time to come to our homes or even visit with us for long in their office.

There are no more Dr. Mooneys. I'm just glad I had him in my life when I did.

Though **Judith Houska** spent most of her adult life in Portland, Maine, she grew up in rural South Dakota, where there were many miles between towns and children had a vast landscape to explore. She has written about many of her childhood experiences, sharing them mostly with her grandchildren, who sometimes accuse her of exaggerating. She isn't.

THE SCHOOL OF HARD KNOCKS
Ruth Jochims

It was hot and sticky, like bees swarming around honey, the summer of 1961. I wore my coolest clothes, shorts, and at night my favorite baby doll pajamas. Many nights my sister and I slept on the living room floor, lulled to sleep by the breeze of the fan.

I was trying to save money for college. I had been babysitting, but people didn't always pay me. They gave me promises they didn't keep, so I finally quit.

One day, a friend of my mother's asked if I'd be interested in a house cleaning job. A woman she worked with needed someone to do some cleaning. I actually liked cleaning other people's houses better than I liked cleaning our own house, so I told her I would.

The next day the man of the house came to interview me. Mr. Marks was retired and had health problems, so he couldn't help his wife with the cleaning. He was friendly, and it was agreed that he would pick me up the next day and bring me home later when I had finished cleaning.

The next day, Mr. Marks showed me a cleaning list his wife had left for me. One of the chores was washing windows. I cleaned inside first, dusting and scrubbing until everything sparkled. When I was ready to do the windows, Mr. Marks showed me a step ladder that was leaning against the house. Since it was so hot, he poured each of us a tall glass of lemonade. He said I should drink it before I went out in the hot sun.

I didn't care for his lemonade. It tasted different than any lemonade I'd ever had, but I drank it to be polite.

There were a lot of windows to clean. The sun beat down on me like an oven as the sweat poured down my face. After a while, Mr. Marks called me in for another drink of lemonade. I was thirsty, so I complied. I drank quickly as he chattered away, and then went back outside to finish the windows.

Soon Mr. Marks was at the door, calling me in for another drink. This drink didn't go down so fast. I felt dizzy. I said something about a funny taste, but Mr. Marks claimed it was just lemonade. It was the strangest lemonade I'd ever had!

When I went outside to finish the windows I had to be very careful because I was so dizzy. Mr. Marks called me in for another drink, but I told him I wanted to finish my work outside.

When I was through with the windows, I went inside and Mr. Marks offered me another drink. I refused it. By now I was suspicious.

"It's just lemonade," Mr. Marks said. "Don't you like lemonade?"

"Not really," I said. Not his, anyway.

Then Mr. Marks came up behind me and put his hand up my blouse.

I jerked away. "Don't!" I said sharply.

He drove me home soon after. I could hardly keep my eyes open. I felt tipsy as I carefully navigated the front steps at my house. Mom met me at the door. "Ruth! What have you been drinking?"

I told her what happened. I went upstairs to my bedroom and lay on the bed, my head spinning.

I was supposed to go with our neighbors to their daughter's graduation later that day. Finally I got up and dressed for the occasion, putting on high heels.

Mom looked at me dubiously. "Ruthie, I don't know about you going—especially in your high heels."

But the neighbors were there and ready to leave. "Oh, I'll be okay, Mom."

Mom was right. I should have stayed home. I'm sure my wobbliness and giddiness was an embarrassment to our neighbors as I precariously navigated the bleachers in the high school gymnasium.

My father had been in a car accident about that time and was in the hospital. If he'd been home I'm sure he wouldn't have let me go back to clean at that house again. Mom certainly didn't want me to go. "That man is crazy!" she said. She called the friend who had recommended the job, and the friend called Mrs. Marks, who said her husband would never do such a thing.

But I needed the money and I promised Mom it would only be for one more day. I also promised them I wouldn't drink anything Mr. Marks gave me.

The next day, Mr. Marks did try to give me lemonade, but I told him I just wanted water.

"There's nothing in the lemonade," he said.

I didn't believe him, and I didn't go back again after that. I had learned a lesson from the school of hard knocks!

Ruth Jochims lives in Centerville, Iowa with her spoiled black cat, Bailey. She enjoys writing and playing the piano and organ.

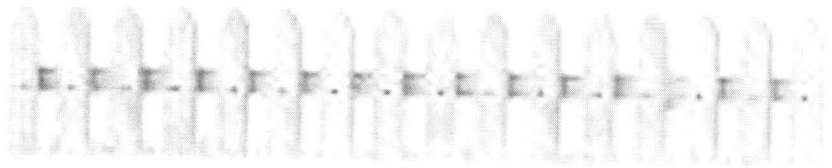

Photo provided by Suzanne Fellows

MY SUMMER AS A CAR HOP

Suzanne Fellows

In 1957 I turned 16, and I was ready to get my first real job. No more babysitting and mowing lawns for me! Granger's Drive-In Diner was *the* place to go in our mid-size Wisconsin city. It featured carhops—girls who would go out to the cars to take orders, then a short while later take the food on a tray back to the car, where the tray would be positioned carefully on the door of the car. Many of the carhops worked on foot, but if you felt secure enough to carry those heavy trays while on roller skates, all the better.

That's what I wanted to do! My mother expressed some concern at first, certain I would fall and break a leg. But I promised I'd be careful and reminded her I'd been roller skating up and down our street since I was five. She relented, and I walked the mile and a half to Granger's to fill out an application.

I was hired, but my first shock came when I learned I would have to supply my own skates. That Saturday I went with Mom to

Oshkosh, where we usually did our shopping, along with my younger brothers Craig and Marc.

First we stopped at the A & P, where Mom picked up a few things on her grocery list. There was a small grocery store in our town, but to get Dad's favorite pork chops—for 63 cents a pound—we had to travel a little farther. Next we stopped at the Oshkosh library where Marc checked out *Old Yeller*, and Craig, who was in his science fiction phase, picked up two books by Ray Bradbury.

At last we went to the sporting goods store. Marc needed a baseball glove for little league that would be starting in a couple of weeks, so Mom bought that first while I looked at rows and rows of skates. In the past I'd only had the adjustable metal skates, the type that fit on the bottom of the shoes and held in place by straps. But for my job at Granger's I would need shoe skates.

I found just what I wanted. Pure white, they laced all the way up in front and had a rubber bumper just below the toe that acted as a brake. They felt good when I tried them on and they were beautiful, but the price tag of—gulp—sixteen dollars was more than I had expected to spend, and more than I had with me.

Mom was sympathetic, but after buying groceries and Marc's glove, she didn't have much left either. She suggested I get a cheaper pair, and pointed out some that were only ten dollars. The shoe skates she was pointing to couldn't compare to the pair I'd set my heart on. It was like test-driving a Cadillac and then being told you could only have an Edsel. But to my surprise, my little brother Marc came to the rescue. He handed his new glove to Mom and said there was still plenty of time before he would need it, for her to use the money for my skates. I hugged him.

My first day on the job I walked to the drive-in with my new skates still in their box, tucked under one arm. Once I was there, the manager told me I'd be under the apprenticeship of Gloria, who always trained the new waitresses. Gloria gave me a menu to memorize, showed me around the place, and instructed me on how to take orders and pick them up.

To my disappointment, Gloria wouldn't let me work while wearing my skates. I had to prove myself on foot first, she explained, for at least a week.

So for my first week—couple of weeks, actually—I carhopped on foot, taking orders and watching the girls on skates with envy. Not only were they being paid twenty-five cents an hour more than the other waitresses, they tended to get much bigger tips. When Brenda and Marilyn, the two best roller-skating carhops, zoomed by my envy grew, and neither girl was shy about telling the rest of us how much they'd made in tips.

Every day as I worked I thought about my skates, resting unused in the small locker I'd been given in the waitresses' back room. At the end of each shift, as I changed from my uniform back into my street clothes, I would sigh and pat the skates as though to reassure them it wouldn't be much longer.

I'd made my preference known, and kept reminding Gloria that I'd bought shoe skates especially for the job. Finally, the day came. She told me to put my skates on and meet her outside in five minutes. Giddy with excitement, I went to get my skates, and quickly realized they were very different from the metal, strap-on skates that I was used to.

Wobbling, arms straight out, I rolled over to where Gloria waited for me. She asked if I was sure I was ready for this. I told her yes, even though I kept one hand on a post to steady myself.

She gave me some time to get my bearing on the skates before handing me an empty tray to practice with. Gradually she loaded the tray with first one plastic mug, then more mugs and some plastic plates, and had me practice some more. Smart move. The mugs and plates took numerous spills before she felt I was ready to work with more breakable ware. Brenda, Marilyn, and the other carhops called out words of encouragement.

Near the end of the day, Gloria sighed and said I was about as ready as I'd ever be. She went out to a couple of cars that had pulled up and were waiting for service. I watched as she leaned down to the driver of first one car, then the other. At the second car she waved at me to come over.

Nervously, trying not to look unsteady on my skates, I took the order of the elderly couple sitting in their Studebaker, and understood why Gloria had me start there—they wanted only one root beer float to share. I wrote it down in my ticket book, rolled back into the restaurant and made the float. A couple of minutes later it felt as though every eye inside and outside of the restaurant was on me as I roller-skated slowly to the Studebaker. Very, *very* slowly.

Those first few days as a roller-skating carhop brought some close calls, but I didn't break anything and before long I was zipping around with the best of them. I worked all summer at Granger's, until the temperature dropped and the drive-in part was closed for the season. I could have stayed on and worked inside over the winter, but I had school to think about so I hung my skates up, promising I would put them to work again next year.

And I did! I used those skates over the next two summers, until I graduated from high school and found work in an office. But sitting at a desk couldn't compare to being on roller skates, and every once in a while I just couldn't resist driving over to Granger's and ordering a root beer float, or maybe a hot dog and fries.

Suzanne Fellows has lived in Wisconsin most of her life, with only a few years away when her husband was in the military. Married to Harv for more than 40 years, they are the parents of three sons and have five grandchildren. She still has her first pair of precision skates, but hasn't had them on in many years.

Photo provided by Roger Brockshus

RING AROUND THE BATHTUB

Roger Brockshus

What images come to mind when you hear people talking about a Saturday night bath? Is it one of past remembrances, or of recognizing a way of life? Maybe the Saturday night bath could be added to something like a Burma Shave sign or a jingle. For example: "Baseball, Hotdogs, Apple Pie, Saturday Night Baths, and Chevrolet." Has a nice ring to it, doesn't it? At any rate, in my sixty-five years, I have come full circle with Saturday night baths.

My parents were married in November of 1946, following my dad's discharge from the Army. Dad had been a young farmer drafted into the military in the spring of 1942. At about the same time, Mom graduated from high school and enrolled in summer classes at Iowa State Teacher's College. By the time Dad was preparing to go overseas, Mom had accepted a teaching position in a country school. They had become acquainted through youth groups at church and corresponded while he was gone.

Mom boarded with different families while she was teaching, and one summer she worked for my dad's family. On weekends, she'd travel about twelve miles to her parents' farm, take her Saturday night sponge bath, go to church with her family, and on Monday morning start a new week.

When Dad returned home, their acquaintance became a courtship. Sunday night was their special date night, preceded by respective Saturday night baths and church with their families. They were married about a year later. After about five years of marriage and four children, baths were made easier and more frequent with the addition of modern plumbing in their farmhouse.

My older sister Darlene was born in October of 1947, I came along in January of 1949, my brother Glen was born in January of 1950, and my younger sister Carol followed in February of 1951. My earliest recollections of our traditional Saturday night baths were of all four of us in the tub at the same time. Mom would put soap on each of us, and then she'd disappear while we splashed ourselves clean. When she was bathing us, Mom was probably pregnant with my brother Bruce who was born in December of 1952. Mom's two sisters came to her aid on occasion and we got by with a bit more splashing when Aunts Betty and Esther were there. By the time Keith, the last in line, was born in July of 1955, we were each taking our own baths.

As the family got older, and my aunts had families of their own, Mom took us to her parents' place on Saturday afternoons. It was a day we all looked forward to, even Dad. He was busy farming, raising pigs and chickens, and milking cows. Sometimes we helped him, and sometimes it was easier for him if we didn't help. We lived about four miles from my grandparents' house, and they were always happy to see us. There we'd be treated to Aunt Sally cookies and tea, milk, and whatever other goodies might be available.

The best part, however, was yet to come. We didn't have television and wouldn't get it until the Christmas of 1960, but my grandparents had a black and white set that we just loved! It was embarrassing to go to Sunday school and listen to the guys talk about the TV show, *Gunsmoke*. I listened to the show on the radio, but the episodes were never the same!

We took turns bathing in Grandma's tub and then watched TV in our pajamas while lying on the living room carpet. While Dad did chores and Mom ran errands, Grandma and Grandpa Hembd babysat six active grandkids. Everyone seemed happy with the arrangement, especially me. It meant I could talk about *Gunsmoke* episodes with the guys in Sunday school.

I was introduced to a shower when I entered high school. My siblings and I had attended a parochial school for most of our elementary education. The building was an old one room schoolhouse that was finally replaced in 1963, my eighth grade year. We played games during recess time, but had no organized sports. When I got to high school, I tried out for basketball. We practiced during the last period of the day, and took showers after every practice, five days a week. Did I really need a bath on Saturday night too?

The next few years were kind of back and forth on showers and baths. When Rita and I were married, we took jobs about twenty-five miles away from our hometown, and rented a small house with room for only a shower. After that, every house we have lived in has had both a shower and a tub. To this day I enjoy a long, hot bath when I have time, but in a busy world, a shower works well.

When our three children were growing up, I occasionally took on additional shifts at the factory. I also started a small lawn business and finished a college degree by attending night school. Rita worked at her job every day, and cared for the kids every night. When Saturday afternoon came, she would run errands or just get out of the house for a while, and it was up to me to take charge of the Saturday night baths. Rarely did we take our children to their grandparents' house on Saturdays, but we did eat donut holes, drink lemonade and have other snacks while lying on the floor watching bowling on TV.

Our children have given us three grandchildren and three step-grandchildren. Our daughter Hillary has twin daughters who are now four years old. They live an active lifestyle, as both Hillary and her husband Brett are teachers and also do some coaching. They live nearly four hundred miles from us. Melanie and Rey are busy with a new baby son, and Rey has twin sons who live nearby with their mother, as well as a daughter in college. They live one hundred miles from us, as does our unmarried son, Justin, who takes care of his own baths.

When our kids come to visit us, they also want to spend time with their friends, so at times Rita and I are the grandparents who take charge of Saturday night baths. Eating graham crackers, drinking apple juice and having other snacks while lying on the floor watching TV still works. The grandkids don't watch *Gunsmoke*, but Disney offers a lot of good choices.

The last chapter of my life has not yet been written, but I have gone full circle on receiving and giving Saturday night baths. By the time I have great-grandchildren, someone will probably have to bathe me. Good hygiene is only part of this circle. I believe the circle has been completed by the same things it started with—soap, water, and love.

There must be a jingle in there somewhere!

Roger Brockshus and his wife Rita were both born and raised in Ocheyedan, Iowa. They were married in 1972 and have lived in Spirit Lake, Iowa ever since. They have three children, three grandchildren, three step-grandchildren, one dog and two grand-dogs. Their family has a variety of interests, and it's difficult to get them all together at the same time. They are all avid readers and bathe regularly.

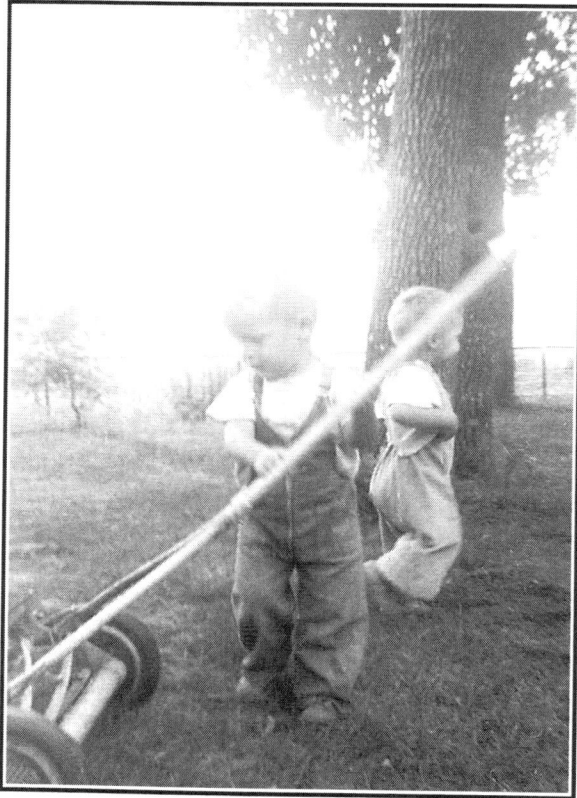

Photo provided by Roger Brockshus

96

MOWING LAWNS ACROSS THE YEARS
Ernie Anderson

Over the years I've mowed many a lawn. Some I was paid for doing, others I wasn't paid because it was for family. But I've seen many lawnmower styles and have worked with most of them.

When I was six, it became my job to mow our front lawn, which was, thankfully, small. This was my first experience mowing, and I used an old push-reel mower. It had no power other than that I supplied, but my dad kept it well oiled, the blades sharp, and it worked well. Back then we didn't care if the clippings stayed on the lawn. They just broke up and went back into the earth anyway.

Our first mower with an engine in it was an Eclipse Rocket Mower. It looked very similar to the reel mower, except it had a small engine perched on top. The first time we fired it up it made so much noise that Smokey, our cat, jumped about a foot in the air, took off and we didn't see her for two days.

The Rocket Mower seemed a revelation to us! For once, my younger brother and I fought over who would get to mow the lawn, instead of who had to. But since he wasn't quite strong enough to get it started with the pull-rope, I usually won that argument. But the novelty soon wore off, and I began to wish for the day when my little brother Bill would be big enough to take over.

By the time I was in high school the power mowers were quieter and were easier to push. I mowed lawns for some of our neighbors as well, and I learned the importance of keeping a mower properly serviced. Our machines were always well-oiled and rust-free.

Next we got a Sears self-propelled mower that Dad had ordered from the catalog. Self-propelled meant we barely even had to push on it to get it to move forward. It had a bag for catching the clippings, which we decided we liked after all. It seemed everyone had power mowers then, and we were even starting to see a few riding lawn mowers around. My brother and I didn't even bother to ask our parents to get one of those. They were frugal, and considered anyone who had to sit down while mowing a lawn too lazy for words.

Mom liked the Sears mower. I left for the Army shortly after we got it, and Bill was involved in every kind of high school sports imaginable, so Mom willingly took over that job. None of us wondered why Dad rarely mowed the lawn. He was busy working, repairing things around the house and keeping our cars in good running order.

That Sears mower was eventually replaced by a John Deere model with the signature green and yellow paint. Mom didn't like that one as much. She said it was hard to push and Dad agreed with her. I had finished my stint in the army by then and Bill was married with a couple of kids, and we both lived within blocks of Mom and Dad so we started taking turns going over there to mow their lawn. Neither Bill nor I thought the John Deere pushed hard and we figured it was just our parents' age that was catching up with them.

Then, when Dad had been retired for a few years, he decided maybe one of those riding mowers wasn't such a bad thing after all. Without telling me, Bill or even Mom, he went shopping, and one morning a shiny new Toro Zero Turn mower was delivered to their house, bright red, with two levers, one on each side of the seat, rather than a steering wheel. Mom took one look at it and announced she would *not* be operating that thing. Bill and I just figured we'd use it to mow our parents' lawn, like we'd been doing for a while anyway, but to our surprised Dad said he would be mowing their lawn himself.

So it happened that, through the course of at least a dozen different lawn mowers over a period of about four decades, our father finally started regularly mowing his own lawn.

Ernie Anderson divides his time between Florrisant, Missouri, where his mother still lives, and the warmer climate of Arizona. The Toro riding mower still runs, though he didn't get to use it for the first time until after his father had passed.

Mennonite barn owned by David Lorch, near May City, Iowa.
David recalls sliding down the berm on his sled, similar to author Kelli
Boylen's account of the haymow hill in her story.

MEMORIES OF THE HAYMOW HILL
Kelli Boylen

When you are a kid, it's pretty easy to think everyone understands your world. While growing up on a dairy farm in Southern Wisconsin, I was rather astounded when, as a teen, I figured out that a whole lot of people have no idea what goes on a farm or where their food comes from.

I remember when a guy from Chicago, who was interested in my sister, came to visit for a day. He had no concept of what might be in a silo. Missiles, anyone? And he couldn't quite get over the fact that the meat we were eating came from our own farm.

There was another time, when I was in Washington DC with the FFA leadership conference program, and we talked to some adults in an elevator who asked what FFA stood for. We explained it stood for Future Farmers of America. They said they'd never heard of it, but that we sure looked nice in our "little blue jackets."

I know now, of course, that people have different life experiences, and even two people growing up in the same place will have different memories of how things were. There are millions of people in this country who have little real knowledge about farms, or what farm life is like.

Recently I had a revelation about my childhood and haymow hills. Now, for city slickers and others who don't know what I'm talking about, a haymow hill is a man-made slope of land that goes to the second story of an older-style barn. The cows were milked downstairs, the hay was stored upstairs, with the hill making it easier to get the hay bales up there.

We had gently rolling hills back home, and that little hill to our haymow was about all there was for an incline. I must have gone up and down our haymow hill hundreds of times with my metal runner sled. When I was older we would pull the sled behind our old clunker snowmobile, but the primary winter activity I remember from being a kid is sledding on that little hill.

I was thinking about how freestall barns offer a lot of comfort to the cows, and milking parlors are great for both farmers and cows, but maybe farm kids today don't always have a place to sled because they don't have a haymow hill. Then I started to look around at the older barns in Northeast Iowa, where I currently live. There are a couple of barns with "hills" to the second level haymows, but, geez, don't I recall nearly everyone back where I grew up as having them? Maybe, since I grew up in an area that was predominantly Swiss, it was something from the Old Country.

I started thinking harder about it. As far as haymow hills go, ours was a little too steep to easily back a hay wagon onto it to be unloaded, so it wasn't very practical for its intended use. But it sure made for good sledding. It also made it easy for a person to get onto the milk house roof with a five-gallon bucket of water to pour on someone exiting the barn in order to start a huge summer water fight.

I Googled "haymow hill" and found only a couple of decent entries among the 100 or so summaries that popped up. These referred to barns built on hillsides so one side of the barn was open to the first level and the other side opened directly to the hayloft, but not any with a man-made hill to the second-story haymow doors.

I did find one bizarre page online that listed the synonyms for haymow as being "anthill, bank, crib, drift, dune, embankment, garner, hayloft, haystack, heap, hill, molehill or mound." The page also had a note stating, "Synonyms are different words with similar or identical meanings and are interchangeable." Well I guess that's another example of the urban-rural gap because we didn't use any of those words for haymow where I grew up.

I guess I was pretty lucky to grow up on a farm with a haymow hill. I hope all children have a place where they can sled in the winter, even if they've never heard of a haymow hill.

Kelli (Kaderly) Boylen grew up on her family's dairy farm in Southern Wisconsin. She now lives in Northeast Iowa with her husband and children. Kelli makes her living as a freelance writer and a licensed massage therapist.

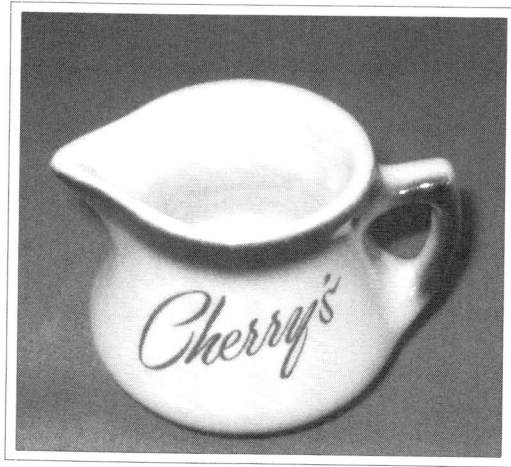

THE DAY MY BUDDY ATE A COW

Ken Sineri

It was at the curve by the railroad bridge on Route 44 just south of Ravenna. It was the best restaurant in Northeastern Ohio. It was Cherry's Steakhouse!

The steaks were perfect every time. So were the fried chicken, red snapper, Italian wedding soup, spaghetti with homemade noodles and meatballs. The whole menu was perfect, especially the tossed salads with that light pink dressing and its little slice of pickled beet.

In April 1965, I moved to California and missed the big event, but my buddy, John Polinori, filled me in. You see, Cherry's featured a steak-eating challenge. If you could eat their 10-pound steak in sixty minutes, it was on the house and your name was forever emblazoned on the honor roll near the entrance of the restaurant. He decided he was going to get his name on that plaque.

John eyed the huge steak each time he ate there. He said it was as big as a loaf of bread.

The waitress noticed his interest and said, "Honey, don't even think about it. Bigger men than you have tried and they all failed."

This only seemed to energize John and he decided that he was going to eat a cow that night.

He agreed to the following ground rules:

- Those who take on the challenge are required to pay for the meal in advance. If successful, your money is refunded.
- You have one hour or less to eat the entire meal consisting of the steak, ranch beans, bread roll with butter, baked potato, and a salad. You pay for your own drinks.
- The entire meal must be eaten and if any part isn't, you lose!
- The 10-pound steak is cooked to your preference, and you are seated at a table for one on a raised platform in the middle of the main dining room.
- Before the timer starts, you are allowed to cut into the steak, and take one bite. If it's to your satisfaction the clock will start. You don't have to eat the fat, but it will be checked.
- Once started, you will be disqualified if you stand up, leave your table, or have anyone else touch the meal.
- If you become ill, the contest is over... YOU LOSE!
- If you can't finish, you are welcome to take the leftovers home with you. However, no sharing of the leftovers is allowed in the restaurant once the contest is over.

As John later told me, he started cutting up the steak and chewing away. But the clock was ticking faster than he could chew. He had to chew harder, faster, faster.

He also said that he probably shouldn't have had those three beers.

He told me, "I was down to my last bite and I didn't have any room left. I forced it down my throat seconds before the alarm went off, There were cheers. I struggled to my feet and painfully waddled into the men's room. I almost made it but not quite. I puked all over the toilet."

Even though he threw up, John still had it down when the alarm went off. He had won. He was famous, and his name would be on the bronze plaque for the whole world to see.

Weeks later, while writing a check at a hardware store, the cashier noticed his name and asked if he was the same John Polinori that had eaten the ten-pounder at Cherry's Steakhouse. She said she had seen his name on the plaque at the front of the restaurant. She wanted his autograph.

John was a bona fide celebrity.

Then suddenly, on October 10, 1965, Cherry's Steakhouse was gone, along with the plaque bearing John's name. Some said it was a leaky gas pipe, but many suspected the Mafia. After all, this was their territory back then. There was always a Cadillac blowing up somewhere.

But John had kept a remaining souvenir of that fateful day at the steak house. He'd suffered an umbilical hernia and ruptured his belly button. What had been an INNIE, now is an OUTIE.

Ken Sineri is a retired mechanical engineer originally from Alliance, Ohio. He has always been a teller of jokes and funny stories that have happened to him, and many of his friends have suggested he should write a book of his adventures. He thought that was funnier than his jokes, until he submitted a story about his first impression of Orange County, California. It was published in the *Orange County Register*, November 2005, and he was hooked. He has written almost three-hundred mostly true, mostly humorous, short stories. He would never be able to do any of this without Bill Gates' spell check and MS Word.

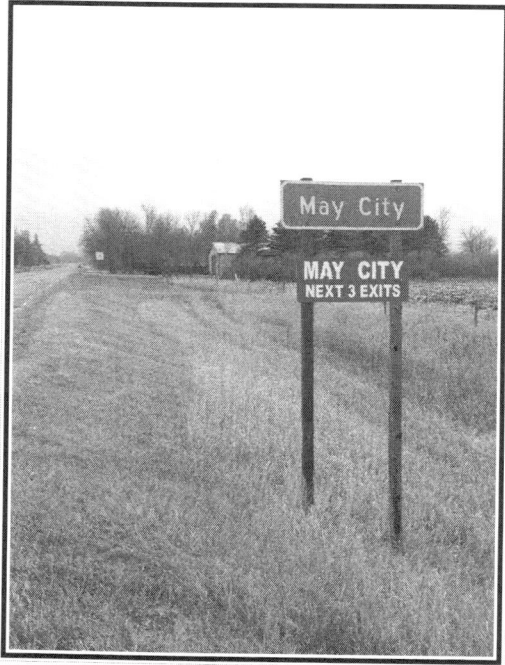

UNCLE BILL

Janet Branson

Uncle Bill was my dad's brother and the youngest in the family. He was eleven years old when the family moved from Chicago to homestead in Montana. They lived so far from any school that he wasn't able to continue his education; as a result, he went only as far as sixth grade.

The three brothers got along well. In fact, Uncle Bill, who was only fifteen or sixteen years old at the time, helped my dad build the log barn that still sits on The Ranch property south of Melstone. The Maart boys loved a good time—you have only to look at their earlier pictures to determine that.

Uncle Bill was quite a character, and he loved to tease. When I was young, he sometimes would just show up at our place in the summer. Not every summer, but I remember a few times when he was there. He liked to help Daddy with the farm work.

One day, when we'd finished eating dinner, it was time for fresh, ice-cold watermelon for dessert. In our family, when we ate watermelon we would cut out the heart of the slice and set it aside to save until we'd finished the rest of the piece.

"Save the best till last," Daddy always said.

On that day, Uncle Bill sat beside my younger brother, Jerry, at the table. As usual, Jerry cut the heart out of his slice and set it aside on his plate for later. But Uncle Bill distracted him somehow, and when Jerry turned his head, Uncle Bill speared the chunk of melon and plopped it into his mouth. When Jerry turned back, his extra-sweet piece of watermelon was gone. Jerry started crying and wailing.

We all knew where it had gone, but Mom was standing behind the table with her back to us and hadn't seen what had happened. When she learned that Uncle Bill had not only taken it, but also eaten it . . . well, she was NOT happy. Uncle Bill never tried that again, not at our house.

I don't think Mom cared for him much, but she tolerated him. Another time when Uncle Bill came, he brought a six-pack of beer. Humph! Mom told him he would have to leave it out in the barn. Nobody was going to put beer in her refrigerator!

Another vice of Uncle Bill's were his cigarettes, and he rolled his own. By this time Jerry and I were eight and ten respectively, and we liked to watch him shake the tobacco out of the tiny Bull Durham sack and onto the cigarette paper. He would spread it out just so, then lick the edge to seal it and twist the ends. We loved the whole process.

But he couldn't smoke in the house, so he would sit outside on the cellar door to roll his cigarette and smoke it. We'd follow him around and we always wanted to know, "How come you smoke those cigarettes, Uncle Bill?"

"Oh, they taste so good," he'd say.

One day Jerry asked, "Can we try it?"

"Sure," he said, and handed his cigarette to us and we each took a puff.

"Oh!"—cough, cough—"That's terrible, Uncle Bill!"

"Well, you kinda have to get used to it, then you'll like it. Maybe you'd like the store-bought cigarettes. They taste better."

"Do you have any we could try?" I asked excitedly.

"No, but the next time we go to town, I'll get some and you can try one."

That sounded good to us, so the next time we went to town we could hardly wait to see if Uncle Bill had bought some of those special cigarettes. Back home again, we waited until he was outside and out of Mom's view, knowing intuitively that this was something she wouldn't like.

"Uncle Bill, did you get some of those store-bought cigarettes?" I whispered.

"Yup, I sure did."

"Can we try 'em?"

"Well, I think we'd better wait a little. We'll try 'em after a while."

Jerry and I couldn't wait. We just knew they'd be good. We found him later out behind the chicken house, and Jerry asked, "Uncle Bill, can we try those store-bought cigarettes now?"

"Sure, come on over here and we'll try 'em."

He made a big show of taking one out of the pack and lighting up. He took a couple puffs, then sighed and handed it to us. "Here you go. Take a nice big puff. It's really good. You'll like it."

Jerry took a cigarette with great anticipation. This one was going to be much better than the roll-your-own kind. He took a puff and passed it on to me. We both began to cough and sputter and gag. "Uncle Bill, that thing tastes terrible too!" I declared.

I'm sure Uncle Bill laughed and laughed about it later. If our mother had learned that he was tempting us with cigarettes, he would have been on the next bus back home.

She never found out. We never told her. Kinda too bad, really.

Janet Branson is a retired school cook. She joined the writers group in Hartley, Iowa, the winter following her retirement for something to get her out of the house. While writing stories about her growing-up years, she discovered writing is fun, and now they can't get rid of her.

BUGGY

Courtney Upah

Around second grade I learned about caterpillars. Our class was shown pictures that explained metamorphosis, and a plant called milkweed that caterpillars liked to eat. We also learned what the different butterflies looked like.

Ever since I was three my family had lived in the same house, one with a cornfield just off the backyard. I loved being outside and exploring, and after that lesson about nature, I realized there was some milkweed right by the field.

Then I hatched a wonderful plan.

After that, I'd go outside often to check the plants for caterpillars or to see if there were any marks that looked like caterpillars had been there. Finally after a few days I found a caterpillar that was striped with yellow, black, and white. I was so excited that I scooped the critter up and put it in a bug house. I grabbed some grass, leaves, and sticks so the little guy would feel more at home, and kept him in my room to keep an eye on him, my little buggy friend.

Each day after school I would race home and go to my room to see if Buggy was eating all right or starting to make a chrysalis. I always made sure the little guy had fresh leaves and grass so he would feel more at home and maybe move around more. I would try different leaves and grass to make sure Buggy was properly fed and cared for.

I was simply astounded when one day I came home and saw that my caterpillar had metamorphosed into a pupa and encased itself inside a chrysalis. I stared at Buggy in wonder, happy that he was growing and all of my hard work was paying off.

I then continued the same routine as before, racing home to Buggy, not wanting to miss his coming out as a butterfly. I didn't move the bug house because there was no longer any need to put fresh leaves in it, and I couldn't stand the thought of anything disturbing Buggy. The little guy didn't move for what felt like a month, but I kept an eye on him the whole time.

The exterior of the chrysalis started out as foggy white, but as the metamorphosis progressed it became clear and I could see that Buggy had orange wings. He was a Monarch!

Once I could see he was almost ready to come out, I would make any excuse to go to my room to check on the little guy.

I was so happy that I was home when Buggy finally decided to emerge. As he stretched his lovely wings, it kind of made me sad because I knew I wouldn't get to keep him and would miss taking care of my little Buggy.

As a family, my parents, brother and I, decided that we would let him out in the backyard. We wanted him to be free. So a short time after Buggy became a butterfly, we all gathered outside. I opened the door of the bug house, but Buggy didn't walk out. I carefully lifted him out, and he fluttered off into the wind.

We watched Buggy go. All he left behind in the cage was the dried chrysalis.

A couple of years later the milkweed behind our house was cut down. No more caterpillars, but life went on. I liked to think about Buggy flying free, and that was good enough for me.

Courtney Upah is a 20-year-old writer/college student, currently studying at Wayne State College. She was born and raised in Iowa.

Photo provided by Jean Tennant

THE BUG AND I

Jean Tennant

It wasn't my first car, but the little VW Beetle was definitely one of my favorites. In fact I've often wished I'd kept it, as it would be quite a collector's item now.

It was a 1970 model, baby blue, just a few years old when I bought it. The engine was in the rear, with the trunk, containing the spare tire, in front. The interior was black vinyl, with front bucket seats, just enough room in back for two people—with their knees up to their chins—and a four-on-the floor stick shift that moved in an H-pattern. The center line of the H was neutral, and to get it into reverse the driver had to press down on the shifter in that neutral line and move it down into the left leg of the H. For a while, when it was having transmission trouble, I couldn't get the VW into reverse so I would put it in neutral, then get out and push it backwards until I was out of whatever parking space I'd found myself trapped.

A downside to the Volkswagen was its lousy heater. I'm not sure it could even have been called a heater. During the winters I kept an ice scraper on the front seat, and if it was cold enough outside I would use the scraper to scrape the frost off the *inside* of the windshield, often as I was driving.

But back then gas was cheap, and the VW was an economical little car. I would routinely pull up to the gas pump and request "A dollar's worth, please." There were no self-serve pumps. An attendant put the gas in, cleaned the windshield and usually checked the oil as well—even for such a paltry amount. On that dollar I would drive most of the week. Sometimes, though, if I was expecting to go out of town, I'd fill the tank—which might cost me as much as seven or eight dollars, depending on how low it had been to start with.

On one such excursion I learned firsthand—in the most foolish way possible—just how robust the VW was. At the same time my good opinion of the people of Iowa was also reinforced.

Karen, a friend of mine, had been to Florida visiting family and she'd asked me to pick her up at the Sioux Falls airport, with her plane arriving at midnight. Though I was well ahead of schedule, it was full dark as I drove along on Highway 9 toward Sioux Falls.

That's when the oil light on the dash of my car came on. I hadn't seen another car in what seemed like ages. The nearest town, which I'd just passed, was Lester, a tiny little burg that had seemed barely a blur as I'd gone past. Now I looked at the glowing oil light, slowing down a bit as I contemplated my options—keep going and try to get to Sioux Falls, or turn around and go back to Lester? Before I could decide, the engine quit entirely and I coasted onto the shoulder of the road.

I put the car in Park, removed the key from the ignition, hooked my purse over my shoulder and started walking nervously back in the direction of Lester. I needed to find a pay phone.

I didn't walk far. Before long a pickup, headed in the same direction, slowed to a crawl and a young woman rolled down the passenger-side window. Another woman was behind the wheel. "You need a ride?" the passenger asked.

You bet I did! She scooted over and I got in the front seat with them. A few minutes later they dropped me off at Louie's Café, where I made my way to the pay phone on the far wall. After dropping in a dime, I made a collect call home, distressed about my car breaking down, Karen arriving soon at the airport and expecting a ride home, etc. What was I going to do?

We were discussing a course of action when a man of about forty approached me.

"Excuse me," he said. "We couldn't help hearing. We'll give you a ride to the airport to pick up your friend, if you want."

"Um... 'we'?" I asked.

"Me and my wife," he said, and I then noticed the woman standing behind him.

"Are you sure?" I couldn't believe my luck.

"Sure," he said. And thus I was introduced to John and Eunice McCarty.

There were plenty of other people in the room, many of who could clearly hear our exchange, so I figured I wasn't likely to go with this couple and disappear without a trace. I left the café with the McCartys.

The plane was just landing when we arrived at the airport. Karen was justifiably puzzled when I introduced her to the Good Samaritans, who then insisted on driving us all the way back to Spencer, and refused to take any money for gas.

It was a few days later before I got back to my car, which by then John McCarty had pulled off the road and to their house. But in the light of day we saw a clearly visible, long streak of oil on the highway, leading right to where the engine had finally seized up. As it turned out, a bolt had worked loose on the oil pan and all of the oil had drained out onto the road.

We fixed the leak, put a couple of cans of oil into the engine, and I held my breath as I turned the key in the ignition. The car shuddered, sputtered and belched out a big plume of black smoke—and started.

I drove that Beetle for another couple of years before trading it off. I've never heard of any car that could be driven without oil to the point of freezing up, without the engine being destroyed in the process. But the VW Beetle was an incredibly tough little car that proved its value in a bad situation.

Just like the small-town couple who went above and beyond to help out a stranded motorist on dark night in the middle of nowhere.

Though author/publisher **Jean Tennant** still calls San Diego her hometown, she has been in northwest Iowa longer than anywhere else. The reason she stays is simple: It's a great place to live!

Photo courtesy of Kiron Kountry. Russell Gustafson family

BUCKIN' HAY
Bonnie Ewoldt

When I was growing up on the farm, few times were more stressful than haying season and few implements more dangerous than a booster buck. This made for a hazardous and sometimes deadly combination, but putting up enough hay to carry the cattle through the winter was crucial, and many farmers stacked hay with booster bucks. My dad owned one in partnership with my brothers.

A booster buck was a wooden apparatus bolted to the frame of the tractor. The motor was a complicated series of belts and pulleys. It operated steel cables that moved the front of the buck up and down.

A high wooden tower above the tractor supported a 14-foot rack-like contraption of pointed wooden slats at the front and a fence-like stop at the back. This device enabled the buck to scoop up loose hay as it skimmed along the windrows. When full, the rack delivered a bundle of hay to the stack where men with pitchforks waited at the top to handle each bundle after the buck pushed it forward off the rack.

Fastening a booster buck to a tractor was difficult, so many farmers dedicated one tractor to the buck and left it attached from season to season. Our buck sat on an old F-20 Farmall, a tractor notorious for rolling over due to the narrow front-end and hand brakes operated by levers located on both sides of the steering wheel. The driver needed both hands to activate the brakes, and this meant no hands remained on the steering wheel! Considering the weight of the hay in a raised booster buck, the center of gravity was somewhere far above the already unsafe front wheels, making the entire process of lifting hay an accident waiting to happen.

The dangerous Farmall, combined with exposed gears and frayed steel cables of the buck, created a hazardous situation, not only in the field, but also on the road. Most bucks were moved from farm to farm during the season. Top highway speed for an F-20 was four-plus miles-per-hour, an insufferably slow speed for farmers waiting to get a hay crop in before the next rain. To speed things up, some buck drivers would take it out of gear on the crest of hills and coast down, with the fourteen-foot wide rack swaying in the wind. The rack was often too wide to clear the county bridges, so it was raised above the side rails, and the tractor was driven down the middle of the bridge with the rack hanging over both sides of the bridge. As if all of this wasn't enough of a road hazard, drivers usually moved their bucks in the evening after a long day of stacking hay so the next job could begin early the next morning.

Dad hired extra help to work the stack, usually high school boys. My husband remembers his days of buckin' hay with tender words like "sweaty, dirty, itchy, sunburned, thirsty, and tempers flaring," and says he was paid one dollar per hour for this hard work. In the heat of a scorching Iowa summer, stackers wore leather shoes and gloves, jeans, and no shirts. Oblivious to the dangers of the booster buck, I remember the haying season as the glory days of summer—a time when I helped Mom with mountains of food and enjoyed flirting with boys in the shade of the haystack while we took lunch to the field. But I digress....

Getting the hay from the field to the top of the stack was an involved process. When delivering a rack of hay, the driver started raising the booster buck while approaching the stack, stopping exactly when the rack was even with the top and before the tractor crashed into the stacked hay. If he didn't stop the lift in time, or if a cable broke or a clutch stuck, bad things could happen. This was even more dangerous because the driver was unable to see the men because of the buck, and they couldn't see him over the edge of the stack. In addition, the load was top-heavy and any unexpected bump could cause the entire load to shift and topple over.

Two or three men worked on top of the stack, using pitchforks to move the hay and keep the stack level. It took the better part of a day to build a haystack, beginning in the morning as soon as the dew was off and sometimes working until dark.

The difficulty of the job was directly proportional to the skill of the booster buck driver. An inept operator would drive the buck directly down the windrow, knotting the hay as it rolled onto the rack. When this happened, the men on the stack needed to tear the knotted hay apart before they could stack it. At other times, an incompetent driver might gouge the dirt and break a wooden buck tooth. Time was lost and tempers flared.

My brother, Russell, was a skilled booster buck driver and created nice bundles while gathering the hay. He was also able to put the buck exactly where the men needed it on the stack—when he was so inclined. At times, he would purposely unload at the opposite side of the stack from where the hay was needed. This doubled their work, but he never heard their expletives as he raced off, laughing, for the next load.

I remember once when Russell pulled a dirty trick. As he brought a new bundle of hay to the top of the stack, a long black snake hung down from it, swaying under the rack. Dad happened to be working the stack that afternoon, and saw the snake as it came up over the edge with the new load. Scared to death of snakes, Dad ran to the edge of the stack and slid to the ground. From there, he jumped into his nearby pick-up and left for town. The men were hysterical with laughter, especially when everyone realized the snake was only a piece of garden hose. Dad never lived that one down.

In spite of the difficult and dangerous work, there were lighter moments during the days of buckin' hay. Miraculously, there were no serious injuries with our booster buck, but stories abound of farmers who were injured and even killed with them. Thankfully, today booster bucks are found only in museums. Still, they were a vital part of farm history, and I have the utmost respect for the invention and the farmers who had the courage to use them for buckin' hay.

Bonnie Ewoldt enjoys writing about being a farm kid in Iowa in the '50s. Several of her stories have appeared in the Midwest Anthology series, as well as Country and Country Extra magazines. More about Bonnie and a collection of her work can be found on her blog: www.bonniesblogbox.wordpress.com.

Photo provided by Judy Taber

THE SKIRT

Judy Taber

I turned ten in the summer and was old enough to join 4-H. That was a milestone for me, as I would be eligible to exhibit the items I'd made at the upcoming Dickinson County Fair in Spirit Lake. The fair was always the first full week in August and ran from Monday through Thursday. It was an exciting time and I couldn't wait to be a participant.

Each of the girls' 4-H clubs in the county had a booth where they displayed items that the members had made throughout the year. The county committee chose a theme, and each club created a centerpiece decoration to express that theme. Booths were then judged and cash prizes were awarded.

The boys' clubs didn't have booths at that time. Their exhibits were all in the livestock area and were housed in various barns on the fairgrounds. Girls didn't join the boys' clubs and they didn't show livestock—yet. I was a junior in high school before I was able to join the boys' club in order to exhibit beef animals.

Choice of projects each year for the girls was determined by the state 4-H guidelines on a three-year rotation of sewing projects, cooking projects, and home furnishing projects. Only items in these areas could be exhibited in their year of rotation. Sewing was the area of learning in the year that I joined the Excelsior Everlasting Echoes 4-H Club.

Our club year began in the fall. At my first meeting we were informed that the next month would be a working meeting, and we were to bring three yards of cotton fabric for a gathered skirt. I was so excited! I had learned how to sew a seam on my Grandma Groff's treadle machine, but I'd never made anything that I could wear.

Finally the day came when Mom and I went to the store to get my fabric. The trip was planned along with other errands as we had to travel thirty miles to the nearest fabric store, located in Spencer.

Prints, plaids, stripes, plains—so many choices. Which one did I want? Mom wisely steered me away from plaids.

"You don't want to have to worry about matching plaids when you're learning," she said. "You can match plaids later."

I didn't really like the stripes, and the plain colors were boring. That left the printed fabrics. Finally we decided on a small print in shades of green. It was dark colored, I wouldn't have to match the design, and Mom said it would be practical. I carried the bolt to the counter and told the sales clerk that we wanted three yards.

Mom questioned whether I had to have that much. The fabric was 36" wide. She said two lengths would make a skirt that would be plenty full. I didn't understand what two lengths meant, but was adamant that our leaders had said to buy three yards, so that was what we got. We also bought a zipper, thread, and a matching button for the waistband. I was all set.

The day of the meeting finally came. Mom delivered me to the home of neighbors who had high school girls in 4-H. They would help us beginners. One at a time we stretched our fabric out on the floor. We measured the length of our skirt and added several inches to allow for a hem. Then we cut our fabric into three pieces that would be sewn back together. For the life of me I couldn't figure out why we had to cut it and then sew it back together again. It seemed as ridiculous as selling swim suits to Eskimos. Why not just put our gathering thread on the long edge and sew that on to the waistband?

They tried to explain about the lengthwise grain of the fabric and that when I cut the pieces, I would be sewing the side edges together, but not at the same place that I had just cut. It still didn't quite make sense to me, but I cut where they told me and sewed the sides of each piece together.

After pressing the seams open, my next task was to put in the zipper. That went smoothly and then it was on to the gathering.

Using a long stitch on the machine, I stitched all the way around my three lengths of fabric to form a gathering thread. Then I began to gather the fabric by pulling one of the threads to slide the fabric together to make gathers. This took a lot of time.

Soon it was time to go home. After being instructed on how to proceed on our own, we gathered up our unfinished skirts, left-over fabric scraps, scissors and thread as our moms arrived to get us.

Mom easily instructed me and soon my skirt was finished. It didn't take long, as she was an accomplished seamstress who made all of my clothes as well as her own.

I put on my new skirt and then twirled and twirled, making all of that fabric float out into a circle around me. I was in heaven. I finally had a *real* full skirt to wear, rather than one made with just enough fabric to do the job.

I took to sewing like a duck to water and was soon making most of my own clothes. It didn't take long for me to learn that I could make several outfits for the cost of purchasing just one, and my wardrobe grew quickly.

After I was married, I did sewing for other people. I made a gazillion bridesmaid's dresses, several wedding dresses (including my own) and even a man's suit. Once I had children in school activities, I phased out of the custom sewing and just sewed for my family.

I taught my daughter to sew but she never wanted to make her own prom dresses. Instead, she would design her dress by combining features from at least three patterns and then say, "Can you make it this way for me?" She ended up with fabulous original dresses for her proms.

Both her junior and senior year, her date arrived to pick her up as I was putting the finishing stitches in her dress.

My last big project was to make five bridesmaids' dresses and my own dress for my daughter's wedding. Again, I was sewing buttons on my jacket at 2 A.M. following rehearsal dinner.

Today my wardrobe consists mainly of jeans and sweatshirts in winter and Capri pants and T-shirts in summer. My sewing skills have mostly been put to rest. However, my ten-year-old granddaughter just joined 4-H. Following her first meeting came the question, "Grandma, can you teach me to sew?"

Judy Taber is retired and lives in a small northwest Iowa town. Growing up on the farm, she continued to sew clothing for many years for herself and her children. Now days she can be found gardening and making stained glass art.

Photo courtesy of Betty Taylor

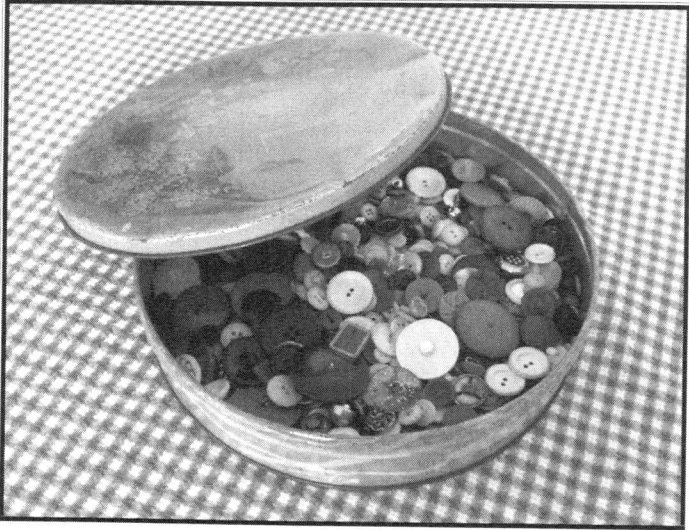

Photo courtesy of Karen Howard

MOTHER'S BUTTON BOX

Karen Howard

Tucked away in the bottom dresser drawer with the snippets of lace from discarded apparel, yards of blue and white ribbon, zippers still in the package, cards of shiny new buttons, spools of thread in a rainbow of colors and assorted patterns, is my mother's button box. It has absolutely no monetary value, but it holds a treasure trove of memories for me.

To be precise, Mother's button box is actually a round, dark lavender tin with scratches, dings and dents, and with a lid displaying pastel spring flowers of tulips, daffodils, lilacs and lily of the valley. The tin started life as a container for decadent chocolates, Mrs. Steven's homemade candies, an extravagant gift from my grandparents to Mother during adverse times.

In an act of old-fashioned frugality, all buttons were snipped from discarded apparel. Before a garment took on its new life as a rag, it was stripped of buttons so they might also have a new life.

In the button box there are shiny black orbs with fancy slides to facilitate removal before washing, colored shank buttons that closed my three sisters' and my dresses, four-hole buttons from the white dress shirts Dad wore to church, and two-hole buttons from his concrete-crusted chambray work shirts. Ordinary white clamshell buttons from the Mississippi River, Bakelite buttons that always melt when ironed, dull olive-drab buttons from worn military fatigues and dress uniforms, and clunky big buttons from winter woolen coats also reside in that battered tin. One and all, they occupy Mother's button box until called upon to replace a lost button or begin service on a new garment. The button box is actually a storybook of days gone by.

When Mother sold the big old house and moved into a retirement village, she gave me the button box. It holds a lifetime's collection of lint, flecks of thread, broken metal zippers, partial sets of snaps, naked cloth-covered buttons with their fasteners long lost, cloth-covered buckles and, of course, the buttons, many of which are a century old. The box is a dumping ground of sewing notions.

Several years ago my friend Diane made me a lovely brooch fashioned from my favorite, more elaborate buttons. It's about the size of the palm of my hand and covered in a collage of dark caramel-colored shank buttons with raised rosebuds in tarnished gold. It's a lapis-colored orb with a surrounding of gold filigree, gold metallic buttons with raised designs, a gold chain, a variegated plume of gold and caramel-colored threads, and a tiny gold heart dotted with a rhinestone. It is an outstanding and treasured piece in my jewelry collection.

I had a favorite dress as a young girl. Mom says I couldn't possibly remember it, at three years of age, but I do! It was a black and brown checkered shirtdress trimmed in white, with Mississippi clam shell buttons sewn with brown thread.

I remember it for several reasons. First, and most important, I could dress myself because the dress buttoned in the front. That was a triumph for a three-year-old. Second, we had a studio portrait taken with me wearing that dress. Third, Mother threw the dress down the basement steps to the ragbag when I outgrew it. I witnessed this offense and commenced to have a hysterical fit, complete with sobbing and kicking. It must have been a lulu of a moment to have lasted this long in my memory!

In the November of 1960, during the presidential election between then-Vice President Richard M. Nixon and the younger John F. Kennedy, Mom was asked to work the voting site in the basement of the Grace Baptist Church. I was called upon to stay home from school and watch my baby sister, Becky. When she was finally down for her afternoon nap, I was free to play with Mother's button box. I set up a classroom. The students' desks were made up of mismatched and dulled shank buttons, and the teacher's desk was a larger brass button with a crest. The crowning glory to this scenario was a lavender shank button that looked like a chalkboard with numbers written on it. The scene was laid out symmetrically on the carpet in front of my dad's big blue leather chair. After nearly fifty-five years, those same buttons used in my classroom are still in the button box, in case I want to play.

The buttons in that battered tin are small but have witnessed an amazing passage of time. They piqued a young girl's imagination and creativity, followed my family's journey thru time and witnessed unbelievable changes in the world. They tell a story to anyone who wants to listen.

Karen Howard is an almost-normal grandma who lives with her dog, Rose, and near her family in Hartley, Iowa. She was introduced to writing by a friend and now hopes to leave stories for her family so that they will know her better and have a written history.

Photo courtesy of Karen Howard

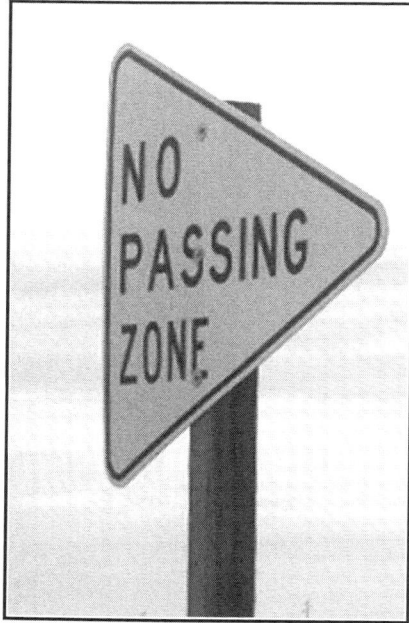

CINNAMON PASS

Karen Jones Schutt

Y husband Charles and I are flatlanders. He was born in Ohio, I in Iowa, and now South Dakota is our home. Granted, these states are not table-flat, but certainly don't compare to the mountains out west. We are like so many other Midwesterners, in that when vacation time rolls around, the mountains beckon. We seem to like visiting land that is more vertical than horizontal, and like experiencing the awe of being able to see far distances from great heights. But when all is said and done, it is good to get back home to the Midwest, with its checkerboard fields, grain elevators, and rich black soil.

And so it was that one summer afternoon found us driving in the Colorado Rockies at the height of tourist season. We decided to take a lesser-known highway to escape the heavy traffic. This led to Lake City where we chanced upon an ornate wooden sign proclaiming the wonders of the road to Cinnamon Pass. The sign also said the Pass was on a road thirty-one miles in length. The road before us was narrow, but smooth blacktop.

"Want to give it a try" asked my husband.

"Sure!" was my enthusiastic reply. There probably wouldn't be many tourists along the way and the road looked equal to our Midwest driving skills.

We followed the road around curves that led higher and higher into the mountains. Abruptly the blacktop came to an end at a large turn-around. Another sign, not ornate at all, ominously informed us the rest of the road, some thirty miles in length, was restricted to four-wheel drive vehicles, no trailers or motor homes allowed. The sign said we must be sure our vehicle was in good working order and have enough fuel to make the trip. Our four-wheel drive diesel pick-up had plenty of power and ten ply tires. It was loaded with a slide-in, pop-up camper, firmly chained to the pick-up. We were fully prepared, both physically and mentally.

The road immediately became rocky and muddy, following the curvature of the land. We encountered very tight switch-backs requiring backing up and going forward two and three times to get around them. The sheer drop-off on the driver's side was dramatic. A great deal of snow was still on the mountains of the Second Range, and snow melt had created incredibly beautiful waterfalls, some only inches wide. Many of these streams were flowing across the road, adding much interest to the drive. I was beginning to feel a little nervous.

As we drove higher, the alpine meadows dazzled us with carpets of wondrous tundra flowers in every color of the rainbow. Some of these flowers were so tiny that a half dozen would fit on a nickel without crowding. Columbine, mountain bluebells, larkspur, asters, and dozens of others made the mountainside a feast for the eyes. And among the flowers were the little trickling streams. Ravens and hummingbirds, along with bees were everywhere.

But I digress.

As I was enjoying the natural flower garden and trying to keep my mind off the road, Charles kept his eyes on the road and fists firmly around the steering wheel. Suddenly at the crest of a hill, he stopped.

"Now, which way does the road go?" he wondered aloud. Looking out the windshield, we could see nothing but space—no road, nothing. I wondered if perhaps we should turn back, but then the drop-off would be on my side and I already knew what the road was like behind us. He opened the door for a better look.

"I think it goes this way," he said, and turned a sharp right. I thought he should have been a little more certain of the direction, but there indeed was the road. I knew there was no logic to my thinking, but I felt safer looking at rocks on my side instead of bottomless space on the other.

We started down fast at a twenty-eight degree angle. (I knew that because I peeked at the gauge on the dashboard.) Charles shifted to super-low and soon we had bounced and jolted our way to the bottom of the slope.

Around a few curves, we descended into a lovely valley. All around were abandoned log cabins and collapsing tipples of old mines. Going east had calmed my jarred nerves a bit. We wandered around and wondered about the history of the place. What on earth were the winters like at this elevation? Too bad we couldn't stay longer, but more exciting roads awaited us.

We began to climb again, with the same kind of switch-backs, the same narrow roads, the same rocks that threatened to tumble us off into the abyss. We did meet some traffic of the quad and jeep variety. They gave us as much room as possible, which wasn't enough for me. I don't like to pass vehicles with half an inch to spare on either side.

Ahead we saw a sign announcing we reached Cinnamon Pass at 14,620 feet. A fierce wind was blowing and snow was banked on both sides. We felt as though we had reached the top of the world.

By now my fingers had formed indentations on the door pull. My feet had almost pushed through the floorboards. I tried not to let Charles know how terrified I was, because if he knew he would tease me unmercifully. So I commented on the beauty around us in a voice that was a bit shrill. He continued to maneuver us downward, shifting now and then, braking, dodging rocks and mud holes.

Finally after hundreds of miles, it seemed, we could see a crossroads in the far distance with outhouses off to the side, a sure sign of civilization. Over more rocks, around a few more tight switch-backs we careened our way downward. When we stopped at a rustic rest area, a friendly fellow traveler said he was concerned about the tilting back and forth of our camper as we had made our way downward. Did he not think, I, too, thought about the whole thing tipping over the mountainside and smashing into a million pieces at the bottom? And what would our kids say?

Farther down the road, now not so rough, we began to see motor homes and large trucks that had obviously come in from the other end. The worst was over. The road widened, we crossed an actual bridge, and we were on blacktop. Around a few more turns and there was Silverton, our destination.

We had started our adventure at 1:15 PM at Lake City and ended at 5:45 PM in Silverton. The trip had taken us thirty-one miles in four and a half hours, which is around seven miles an hour. Most of that time, I thought we were going too fast.

A few days later we were traveling northeast of Gunnison, looking for interesting roads. Using my DeLorme map book, I found a likely road.

As we climbed, I saw that the road on the map continued several pages farther in the book. After turning to that page, I noticed we were on our way up to a place called Cumberland Pass, 14,000 plus feet.

But that's another story.

Karen Jones Schutt is living the good life near Sioux Falls, SD, which means being retired, residing in the country, and keeping track of her children, grandchildren, and especially a new great granddaughter. She and her husband Charles continue to travel to out-of-the-way places in their trusty pickup camper.

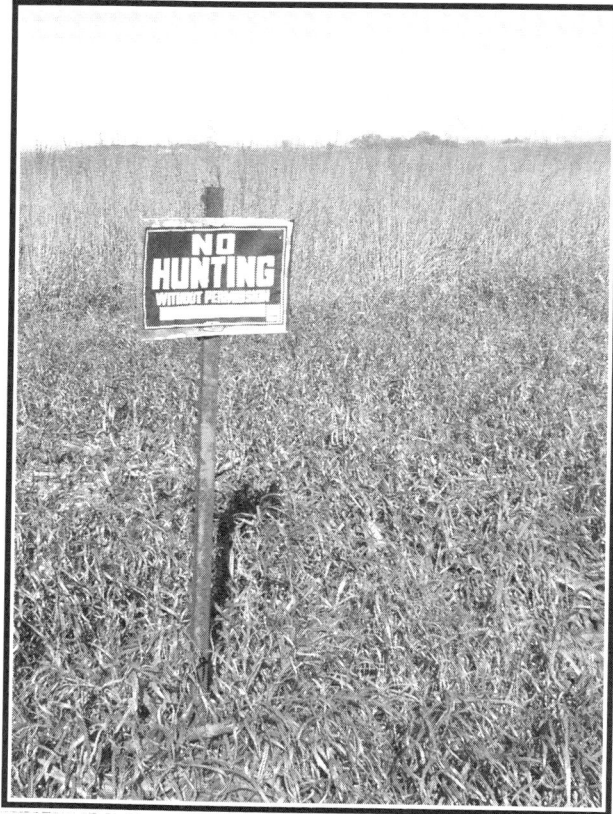

THE INVENTOR
Walter Smith

My father was a tinkerer. Our garage never actually held cars, to my memory, but instead contained a wide array of tools, a couple of worktables, and always at least a half dozen of his projects in various stages of completion. I recall one period of time when the guts of a discarded washing machine sat in one corner of the room, the inner working cannibalized for other projects.

When I say he was a tinkerer, I'm really not doing him justice. My father didn't just putter around fixing broken household items for my mother, though he did that too. No, he was much more than that. Doyle Smith had vision.

At age eight I received a much-coveted new bicycle for Christmas, a beautiful Schwinn Challenger, blue and white, with a single headlamp attached to the handlebars. We'd been experiencing an especially mild winter that year, and I spent the following week riding up and down the street in front of our house. But once school started again after Christmas break, there wasn't enough daylight left by the time I got home to ride my bike.

In stepped Dad. He saw me moping around, wishing for just a little more riding time, and decided to do something about it. Taking parts from an old radio and a couple of filament lamps, he rigged my bike with a set of blinking lights, attached to the front and back fender, which were controlled by a switch on the handlebars. Those blinking lights kept me visible as dusk descended on the neighborhood, and I was allowed to ride my bike until the streetlights came on.

Likewise Dad, using the tub from the aforementioned washing machine, made a dishwasher for Mom. The inside had racks for the dishes, a hose that ran from the kitchen faucet into it, and a turntable inside that sprayed hot water in a circular motion over the dirty dishes. With the first test-run he hadn't yet perfected the water pressure, and some drinking glasses were shattered. After that he practiced with non-breakable plastics until the bugs were worked out and the dishwasher was running to perfection.

Some of his other creations included a sunlamp hat, puncture-proof bicycle tires, an egg poacher that nearly burned our house down and a self-cleaning litter box that our cat refused to go near. I now see similar litter boxes for sale in pet-supply stores everywhere.

Doyle Smith was ahead of his time.

Though my mother urged him to apply for patents on some of his inventions, he never wanted to spend the money needed for the application process. His first priority was his family. A far better investment, he felt, was to save diligently for the college educations of his five children.

One missed opportunity, however, nearly broke all our hearts.

Mom was a big believer in vegetables. A large salad bowl was usually at the center of any meal, holding lettuce, cucumbers, carrots, red onions, and whatever else she had on hand at the time. She also prepared scalloped potatoes, and casseroles thick with tomatoes. After seeing how long it took for Mom to prepare her culinary masterpieces each evening, Dad started looking for a way to simplify the process for her. After a few fits and starts, including one prototype that took a carrot, mutilated it and then jammed so badly that he had to dismantle it, they finally had the perfect kitchen gadget.

Dad called it the Nicer-Slicer.

The Nicer-Slicer was a hand-operated miracle to behold. With the criss-crossing blades inside, safely out of reach of little fingers, Mom had only to place the vegetable of choice between a set of blades, then push down on the top of the device. Cucumbers, peppers, mushrooms—they all shot out of the bottom in perfectly symmetrical slices. A simple adjustment to the blades, put in a raw peeled potato, and in no time at all you had a plateful, ready to be put in a pan of hot oil for fries. It was so much fun that we kids fought over who would use it next.

This time, even Dad couldn't hide his excitement. He talked about patenting the Nicer-Slicer. We were all for it. To heck with college. We'd be rich!

But a few weeks later, just as Dad had begun filling out the patent paperwork, we heard my brother Dennis shout from the direction of the living room. We rushed to see what he was yelling about, and found him standing in front of the television, a stricken expression on his face. He couldn't speak. He just pointed at the TV.

And there it was. A commercial for the Veg-O-Matic. "It slices! It dices!" We saw immediately that the Veg-O-Matic by K-tel was very similar to Dad's Nicer-Slicer, but more streamlined. It was actually—we hated to admit—better.

While the rest of us continued to watch the commercial in horrified fascination, Dad quietly went back to the kitchen. There he picked up his small pile of paperwork and dropped it in the trash.

Dad didn't stop tinkering, but that spark of excitement he'd always had was diminished. It was as though he couldn't allow himself to get his hopes up too much, and risk facing such a disappointment again.

All five of Doyle Smith's kids went to college, but better than that, we were given the gift of being able to examine a problem with a clinical eye and finding a solution of our own making. We all love to tinker. A couple of us even hold patents.

Walter Smith and his family live in Indianapolis, Indiana, where he grew up and where he remembers to this day his father's genius with gadgets. Though he never found wealth or fame, Doyle Smith did eventually patent a few of his ideas, which are still in use today, though on a smaller scale than his children believe his Nicer-Slicer would have been.

Photo provided by Scott Rubsam

OKOBOJI AND BEYOND

Scott Rubsam

I have always loved the theatre. I loved movies too, particularly Walt Disney movies. I saw them all.

I read about the stars in movie magazines, complete with photo layouts and the secrets of their lives. I particularly loved Hayley Mills and Tommy Kirk. I wanted to be one of those child stars. But I lived in Minnesota. And try as I might, I couldn't get my parents to move to Hollywood. As a child star, I could have supported them. But they just didn't see the logic. My movie stardom would have to happen some other way. Somehow I would have to work my way to Hollywood.

So I acted in high school plays. Won the best acting award for my part in *Time Out for Ginger*, and attended the national speech conference, competing against a young Oprah Winfrey. I actually went more rounds than the soon-to-become-billionaire.

Acting professionally was still my dream after high school, but Hollywood was a long way off. There was one professional summer stock company about forty miles away from where I lived. Located in Iowa's Great Lakes region, the Okoboji Summer Theatre had good productions. I wanted to work there.

Every summer the playhouse did nine weekly shows, with professional actors working alongside college students. It wasn't Hollywood, but it was closer than high school. One of the professional actors had appeared in an episode of *The Twilight Zone*—a real, living, working actor who had breathed the star-studded air. I was sure all that success would rub off on me. That Hollywood career and even an Oscar appeared on the horizon, fuzzy at the edges, but still ever so shiny and gold.

From the local newspaper critic, I learned this theatre sometimes hired high school interns from the area to play the smaller roles.

My mother got involved. She peered at me knowingly from behind a pair of stylish black-cat glasses, her jet black hair swept high and piled up on her head. "Send them a letter of intention," she said.

"What should I say?"

"Tell them why you want to work there and what you hope to accomplish by working there." Ever the schoolteacher, her red-pencil editing-whip impatiently waited. "But it has to be well-written. Pour your passion into it. Everybody appreciates a well-written, passionate letter."

So I dashed off a well-written, passionate letter—whisked it off and sat back to wait for their acceptance.

A letter did come back—not well-written or passionate—with a resounding *no*. They were not interested in hiring me, though they acknowledged that occasionally students who lived in the area helped them out.

Well then, I'll live in the area, I decided. So, without any further correspondence, I secured a place in the bathroom of the rehearsal barn, which sat on property not owned by the theatre, across a field and through a fence. The owner of the barn let them rehearse the plays there for free, and he agreed to let me live in the bathroom. Rent free. So with a sleeping bag, some Fritos, a small record player and my high school graduation money, I relocated to the bathroom of said rehearsal barn.

My mother drove me to my lodgings. When it came time for her to go, I was suddenly nervous. "Let's go have dinner. Shrimp cocktail at the Candlelight Supper Club," I suggested.

She looked at me. "It's all yours now. Make yourself proud. " And then I was left standing in the fumes of her beat-up Chevy.

As I unpacked I steadied myself. *This is what you want*, a voice in my head said, just a little too loudly. *The theatre is your life. Make your parents proud.*

But when I showed up and explained I was there to work, the people at the theatre less-than-kindly explained they had nothing for me. "Maybe we'll have something for you in a month. Come back then."

I returned to my bathroom and sat sadly on the bed, munching Fritos. I opened my little portable record player and munched and crunched to Peggy Lee's "Is That All There Is?"

How long did I have before I ran out of Fritos and money? A month, maybe? What was I going to do? I couldn't go home. Home was now the bathroom of a rehearsal barn. I couldn't call my parents and boo-hoo, saying it hadn't worked out. They'd think I was a failure. And so would my friends. My "cool" rating with them was at an all-time high. Going back would destroy that.

Calming my nerves with another handful of Fritos, I gathered more courage than knew I had and wandered back to the theatre. And that's when I met my savior.

Martha Letterman. Gruff-but-with-a-heart-of-gold Martha Letterman. She ran the children's theatre, which housed the experimental theatre as well.

And she was scary.

She sucked hard on a cigarette, spewing smoke from her nostrils like a dragon on loan from a Walt Disney film. She barked at me: "Who are you? What are your qualifications? Do you have a vitae?"

She sized me up, her eyes boring holes into mine. I spilled myself out, telling her who I was, every last friggin' detail, ready with corroborating high school yearbook and library card.

Squinting, she circled me. "Can you stage manage?"

"What's that?" I gulped.

"Can you stage manage? Act as my assistant. Someone who knows the show, who's in charge of the lights, the sound, the costumes, the props." She paused dramatically. "Someone who guards The Book."

"Guards the book?" It sounded like a James Bond movie.

"Yes. The Book." She stood closer, pointing a finger at my chest, exhaling large clouds of stinky air. She was on a roll. "Someone who runs errands. Does what I tell him to do. Shines my shoes when and if I need them shined. Someone who is at my side morning, noon and night." Lots and lots of smoke spewing here. "Someone who can ride a wild horse to the moon and back, if I say to. You game?"

Oh my god, working for a scary, barking, smoking lady with a million questions who might-or-might-not need her shoes shined and some kind of book guarded while riding a wild horse somewhere and back!

But it sounded better than idly eating Fritos all summer. I went to work.

I did a little bit of everything during those months. Once I even substituted in a children's play for a no-show actress, playing a British bird with an accent. Hail Britannia! I was on my way. Unfortunately, said actress came speeding up the next day in a cloud of dust and my British accent disappeared as the dust settled.

But the summer turned out well: acting, stage managing and shadowing a scary, barking lady made a huge impact on me.

At summer's end, I headed off for college with little money, but a suitcase full of knowledge and memories of hard work, tears, laughter, talented people and seemingly never-ending bags of Fritos.

I didn't go to Hollywood, do films or television, or even continue to act. Instead, I went east, landing in Greenwich Village, the heart of New York City where I worked steadily making a living as a director.

I found work in many places over the years: Chicago, London, San Francisco, American Samoa. All I remember about that era was running to catch one plane or another in one city or another. But I was fortunate and happy to have the career that I did. It was a godsend.

All during that busy time, my parents didn't say much about my career. I often wondered what they thought of it. I certainly wasn't a millionaire. Other relatives often asked Mom and Dad, "When is Scott going to get a real job?" I secretly wondered if my parents considered me a failure.

Then, one year I accepted a job directing and teaching at San Diego State University. It was a nice place to work and the sun was great.

I went to San Diego in the summer to set up a home and earn some money before fall classes began. I secured a temp job as executive secretary for an electronics firm that sold parts to various companies around the United States.

One day, I left my name and a message for the head of one of our affiliates. A short while later, he called back. As I rifled through my papers, preparing to ask him some pricing questions, he blurted out: "Is this Scotty Rubsam, son of Maurice and Doris?"

I was dumbfounded. How could he know that? I was a newcomer to the firm, and no one called me Scotty anymore. It was an affectionate name from my past.

I sputtered, "Y-yes."

"Are you still in the theatre?"

"Y-yes, I am," I sputtered again, unbelieving.

"Oh Scott", the man almost whispered, "I've done business with your father for many, many years. He talks about you constantly... where you are, what you're doing. Are you still directing? He brags all about you all the time."

My father had seemed so disinterested in my career, including my fifteen years on the island of Manhattan, working steadily, sometimes with some Oscar-winning actors. I couldn't remember a time he'd expressed much interest in what I did for a living.

The man at the other end of the line continued speaking. "Your parents are so proud of you—that you've worked so hard doing something you love. How many people can say that?"

And with that he placed an order.

Outside the Santa Ana winds roared, picking up the dust and flinging it against the window. I sat at my desk and tried to make sense out of this odd little phone call.

I've been told many times that the universe can come out of left field, delivering information when most needed and least expected, in the most surprising ways. I hadn't believed it. Until then.

Whenever I remember the words of that stranger, I know I am one of the lucky ones. I think back to the summer of 1970 and the Okoboji Summer Theatre, when I was a kid just starting out, when I rode a wild horse to the moon and back.

That summer—and Martha Letterman—made all the difference in the world to a young man with a dream.

Scott. Rubsam has written and directed three scripts for The Guthrie Theater, and has held directing stints at numerous regional theatres around the country including a production of *The School for Scandal* with film and television star Jeanne Tripplehorn. In addition to creating the playwriting program for the San Francisco School of the Arts, he has taught and directed for Duke University, The Dramatists' Guild, University of American Samoa, San Diego State University, Augsburg College, Hamline University and Macalester College and The Walker Arts Center. He is the author of eight plays.

Photo provided by Scott Rubsam

Photo provided by Scott Rubsam

THE END

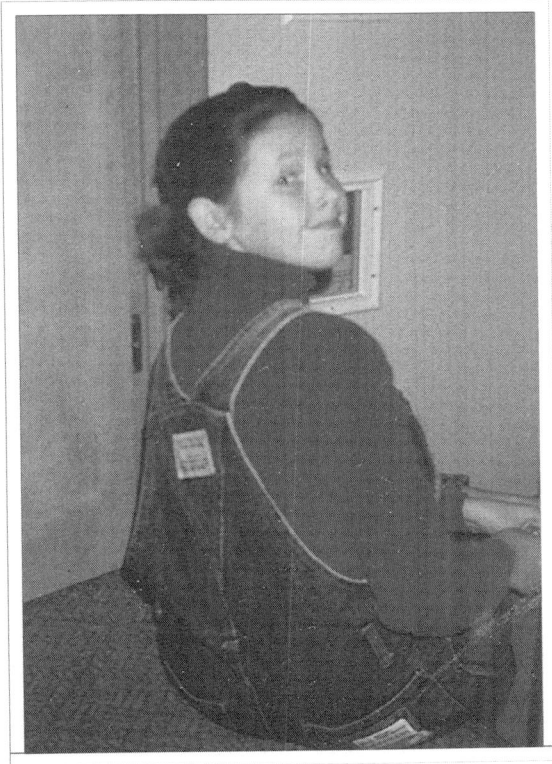

SUBMIT YOUR STORY

The next Midwest anthology—no title yet—is due for publication in late 2015. If you'd like to submit a story for this or future anthologies, here are a few things to keep in mind:

- Send a true, original story of 600 – 1200 words.

- A Microsoft Word document as an email attachment is the preferred method, though submissions by mail—typed, please!—are also accepted.

- The deadline for each anthology is April 30th of the publication year.

- Photographs are welcome. A copy is preferred, but if you send an original it will be scanned and returned to you. Shapato Publishing accepts no responsibility for lost photographs, so be careful about sending those precious family photos.

- Payment for your story if accepted for publication is $25 upon signing of the contract, plus one free copy of the book when available.

Any of these details may change at any time. Nostalgia is always welcome, but so are contemporary stories if they fit in with the general theme of the anthologies, which is upbeat. Send to:

Email: jean@shapatopublishing.com

Mail: Jean Tennant
        Shapato Publishing, LLC
        PO Box 476
        Everly, IA 51338

17002277R00103

Made in the USA
San Bernardino, CA
26 November 2014